BILLY BITZER
His Story

BILLY BITZER

His Story

by

G. W. BITZER

FARRAR, STRAUS AND GIROUX

Contents

Illustrations

(*Those marked * are reproduced by courtesy of the Museum of Modern Art. All others are from the Billy Bitzer Collection, courtesy of Mrs. Bitzer*)

Introduction

by Beaumont Newhall

Billy Bitzer began his career in motion pictures at that critical time when the making of peep-shows for amusement parks and penny arcades was giving way to the production of films to be screened in theaters across the land to more than two million Americans every day. He played a vital role in the shaping of the most powerful visual medium of our time.

When he began working with the Magic Introduction Company in 1894, one of his first assignments was to help in the production of a peep-show motion-picture viewer called the Mutoscope, which, it was hoped, would rival the success of the Kinetoscope, just introduced by Thomas Alva Edison, the "Wizard of Menlo Park."

Inspired by the photographic motion studies of Eadweard Muybridge and Étienne Jules Marey, Edison undertook the project of producing a continuous series of sequential photographs which, when presented to the eye intermittently and at a rapid rate, would reproduce action. He assigned the development of this project to his employee William Kennedy Laurie Dickson. The result was the Kinetoscope: a cabinet loaded with a fifty-foot endless loop of 35 mm film, the edges perforated to fit sprockets in a drum that drove the film past a magnifying glass and a slotted, whirling disk. On looking through an eyepiece, a person saw a diminutive moving image for thirteen seconds. The subjects of these first films were trivial: blacksmiths at work, Anna Belli in her serpentine dance, wrestling, Sandow the Strongman flexing his muscles, and other glimpses into the worlds of vaudeville and sports.

The peep-shows at once became popular. A Kinetoscope Parlor was opened on Broadway, in New York, on April 14, 1894, with ten machines, so that people could look at the films one after another. In May machines were shipped to Chicago, in June to San Francisco, in September to Paris and to London. Each Kinetoscope cost $200. It was good business for Edison, for several machines were required to set up a parlor, and the films, which were sold separately, had to be replaced frequently with fresh subjects.

But the audience for the Kinetoscope was limited to one person at a time for each machine. Inventors and engineers began to devise ingenious projectors that would throw the film images on a screen, where they could be viewed by people seated in an auditorium. By 1895 a host of machines were being demonstrated, and some were in regular use in theaters: Henry Latham's Eidoloscope in Keith's Bijou, New York, in April, and in the Olympic, Chicago, in August; Max Skladanovsky's Bioscop in Berlin's Wintergarten for the entire month of November; the Lumière Brothers' Cinématographe in the Grand Café des Capucines, Paris, beginning December 28.

The Lumière films were a sensation. Georges Méliès, proprietor of the Théâtre Robert-Houdin, described this first show: "I found myself with other guests in front of a little screen just like that used for stereopticon shows, and in a few minutes a still photograph was thrown on it, showing La Place Bellecoeur in Lyon. A little surprised, I said to my companion, 'So they've bothered us to come see lantern slides. I did that ten years ago.' I had hardly finished the sentence when a horse hauling a carriage began to walk toward us, followed by other wagons, then pedestrians; in a word, all the animation of the street. At this sight we sat there with our mouths open, astounded, surprised beyond expression.

"Then followed *The Wall*, broken down in a cloud of dust; the *Arrival of a Train, Baby Eating Soup*, with as a background trees waving in the breeze, then *Workers Leaving the Lumière Factory*, and finally the famous *Hoseman Hosed*. At the end of the show all were delirious, and everyone asked himself how such a result could have been obtained."

Despite enthusiasm for the theatrical presentation of motion pictures, Edison saw no future in it. "If we make this screen picture that you are asking for, we'll spoil everything," he told an associate. "We are making these peep-show machines and selling a lot of them at a good profit. If we put out a screen machine there will be a use for about ten of them in the whole of the United States." But Edison's backers finally persuaded him to buy a projector designed by Thomas Armat. It was put on the market as the Vitascope, and—by agreement with Armat—as Edison's invention. On April 23, 1896, Edison films were projected with it in Koster and Bial's theater in New York City.

On June 29, 1896, Lumière's Cinématographe was shown simultaneously at Eden's Musée and at Keith's Union Square Theater in New York, with a reception that the projectionist, Félix Mesguich, one of the firm's cameramen, described as terrific: "The audience was wild. They shouted 'Lumière Frères!,' 'Lumière Brothers!' and hurrahs were mingled with shrill whistles. . . . Unforgettable! I was sad that the inventors were not present."

W. K. L. Dickson, the inventor of the Kinetoscope, left Edison's employ in 1895. After working for a while perfecting Latham's Eidoloscope, he joined Harry Marvin, E. B. Koopman, and Herman Casler in the invention and development of the Mutoscope. Marvin and Casler were engineers in Canastota, New York; Koopman was proprietor of the Magic Introduction Company—Billy Bitzer's employer.

The Mutoscope was a simple device: one thousand paper photographs printed from a film negative exposed in a motion-picture camera were mounted radially around a drum. This unit was inserted vertically into the machine and caused to revolve by turning a crank. A metal dog, which rode on top of the picture drum, allowed the cards to flick by an eyepiece fitted with a lens. Thus the illusion of motion was created.

If the Mutoscope was simple, the camera that took the pictures was not. To avoid legal interference, each specification in the Edison patents was avoided. The film was 2¾ inches wide instead of 1⅜ inches. It was not perforated and was driven by friction rather than by a sprocket drum. At the moment of exposure two pins were thrust through the film, holding it steady for the fraction of a second that the lens was open. This colossal contraption, which Bitzer so vividly describes, weighed five hundred pounds without the heavy electric storage batteries that powered it.

It was now obvious that the future lay in the projected image and not in the peep-show, and the American Mutoscope Company, as the syndicate became known in 1895, designed a projector which they called the Biograph. Somehow Bitzer managed to operate it at the press preview and at the New York première at the Olympia Theater on October 12, 1896. The company was now in business.

Because the films first made by the American Mutoscope Company were 2¾ inches wide, they could be shown only in the Biograph projector. Therefore, the company offered theaters a package unit, consisting of the selected films, a projector, and a projectionist. Often a Mutoscope camera was taken along as well, despite its bulk, and local scenes and events were photographed by the projectionist, processed on the spot, and shown the same day. But there was little market for this service, since most theaters were equipped with projectors to handle the Edison standard perforated 35 mm film. In 1902 the company built a reduction printer, converted 2,500 subjects to 35 mm "sprocket films," and sold them in twenty-five foot lengths at $5 each.

The American Mutoscope Company, soon popularly known as "Biograph," was now in direct competition with Edison and Vitagraph, a film production company founded in 1899 by J. Stuart Blackton and Albert E. Smith. Blackton had bought a projector from Edison and had converted it into a camera.

Gradually the content of films grew from short takes of current events, vaudeville turns, jokes and pranks, and titillating glimpses of semidressed girls, to narratives. Of these Edison's *The Great Train Robbery*, made in 1903 by Edwin S. Porter, became a popular sensation. During Christmas week that year, it was shown simultaneously in eleven theaters in New York City alone. Chicago reported that during the same week it made the biggest hit of any film shown in the Olympic Theater, and from Denver came news that the Orpheum was holding it over for a second week, "contrary to all precedent." The film was in demand as late as 1907, when the distributor announced that the negative of this "greatest selling film ever made" was worn out and prints could not be supplied.

Small theaters, hastily constructed in empty stores and halls, were opened for the exclusive purpose of screening films. In 1905 two enterprising Pittsburgh men—John P. Harris and Harry Davis—named their store-theater the "Nickelodeon" and opened with *The Great Train Robbery:* they grossed $1,000 per week. The name caught on, and nickelodeons spread across the country. In 1907 it was estimated in *The Saturday Evening Post* that there were over five thousand in the United States and that every day two million people attended them. The nickelodeons were deliberately kept small, with not more than 199 seats, one seat less than the average city's definition of a theater requiring a license of $500 or more. They were open every day of the week from 8 A.M. to midnight.

The motion picture was now an American social phenomenon. The most avid patrons were the slum dwellers, many of whom were recent immigrants ignorant of English. With the silent film there was no language barrier. Children were particularly attracted to the nickelodeons; it was estimated that they made up one-third of the attendance. Social workers feared that the films might have a bad effect upon their morals, but when they investigated, they found the nickelodeons a positive force that might even drive out the saloon. The New York *Morning Telegraph* wrote in 1907 that the investigators of the New York People's Institute found that "the nickelodeons were furnishing upon the whole healthy and even educational amusements to classes which stand sorely in need of it. Many of the amateur sociologists who had long dreamed of a theater within the reach of the means of the very poor were surprised to discover that something very much resembling it had grown up unaided in these shows." Billy Bitzer's account of how the nickelodeon films were used as an audio-visual device to teach foreign-born newcomers English is a contribution to this little-understood era of motion-picture history.

Shows in the nickelodeons were changed twice a week at first, then three times a week, and in 1907 every day—or even twice daily, with a new feature every afternoon and every evening. The demand for films was staggering, and they were turned out by the Biograph team at the rate of one a day. Bitzer made some three hundred films between 1899 and 1908. He had photographed a real war and many staged ones; famous people on location and beautiful actresses in the studio; glorious scenery and absurd comic chases, such as *Personal* and *Lost Child*. His camera would be spurned today, even by a weekend amateur. It was hand-cranked; there was no speed control, and the number of frames per second was a matter of subjective judgment. Exposure was by experience, not by a photoelectric cell. Focusing could be done only before shooting: reflex through-the-lens viewing of the subject was not possible. Yet Bitzer always secured his pictures. His camera was second nature to him, and his love for it is a leitmotif throughout his autobiography.

When David Wark Griffith joined Biograph early in 1908, he did so because he needed work as an actor. Later that year he reluctantly accepted a job as a director. He knew nothing whatever about motion-picture production. It was fortunate for the future of the motion picture that he found the enthusiastic, wholehearted support of one of the most experienced filmmakers of the time, who could show him the camera's capabilities and who could respond positively to his unconventional demands. They formed a brilliant team. Bitzer sums up his contribution to film history in one humble sentence in chapter ten of his absorbing memoirs: "What Mr. Griffith saw in his mind we put on the screen."

BILLY BITZER
His Story

Foreword

When I started out as a cameraman in 1896 the Biograph camera weighed close to a ton. These were the days before movies were ready to be projected on the screen. They could be seen only when the viewer turned a crank and looked into a peep-show machine at the penny arcades. In 1896 at Hammerstein's Olympia Music Hall in New York, I was the projectionist of Biograph's first screening in a theater. We showed pictures of Presidential candidate William McKinley at his Ohio home, which I had taken; of the Empire State Express rounding a bend; of Joseph Jefferson as Rip Van Winkle; and two or three other shorts. *The New York Times* reported next day:

The finest of all these pictures was one of the Empire State Express going at sixty miles speed. The train is seen coming out of a distant smoke cloud that marks the beginning of a curve. The smoke puffs grow denser on the vision, and soon coach after

3

coach whirls to the front, and it seems as though the entire left-hand section of the house [the Olympia] would soon be under the wheels . . . The cheers that greeted the picture and its representation were as great as those for McKinley.

In 1899 I was leading cameraman of the Jim Jeffries–Tom Sharkey fight at the Coney Island Athletic Club. The fight went twenty-five rounds (two hours and ten minutes) and we exposed seven and a half miles of film. A 4.5 lens with an 8-inch focus was used, and the old Biograph film was nearly nine times larger than that used today. The film ran at 320 feet a minute, as compared with 90 feet a minute for today's film.

In 1914, *The Birth of a Nation* was made with the lightweight Pathé camera, which from that time I used exclusively during my years with D. W. Griffith. Though the Bell & Howell camera (a much steadier machine, because it was electrically operated) had just become available, we could not afford it. So the Pathé camera did the job, and a good job too, allowing me to improvise on Griffith's suggestions. It all made for good teamwork. Being pioneers, we were credited with having inventive minds, but it was really a case of necessity being the mother of invention. When we took such scenes as the train hurtling toward the audience, it was considered quite a feat. The fact is that we often learned new tricks through our mistakes. For example, once I happened to film street scenes in mid-Manhattan, only to find when we screened them at the studio that a Hudson River steamer was plowing up Broadway. Only then did I remember that I had put the magazine with the Hudson River shots into a pack of fresh film. From this dumb error I discovered the possibilities of double exposure.

The Birth of a Nation, which changed movie history and swept the country after its release in 1915, was our mortgage-lifter, as it was also for many theaters around the country. When *The Birth* was road-showed, it carried its own complete orchestra, projectionists, sound effects, and sheet music. If a theater had its own projecting machine, it was removed, and for the first time two projectors (ours) were used. We thus eliminated the "One Moment Please" announcement, a familiar sight to patient moviegoers in those days, as they waited between each reel for the projectionist to change over.

The Birth of a Nation was made practically in the back yard of the Reliance-Majestic studio at the corner of Sunset and Hollywood Boulevard. Except for the battle scenes, taken at old Universal Field and some cotton fields in Calexico, and the fir-tree scene, taken at Big Bear, that back yard is where most of Griffith's masterpiece was photographed. The getting together of the money to finance it is another story, but happily the result was that everyone who put money in it (like myself) got it back many times over.

All this reminds me of the spot I always called "the magic carpet"—the rug that covered the lobby of the Alexandria Hotel in Hollywood, where in those days movie people gathered. If anyone had, say, a $30,000 deal, he would step away from the cheap talk at the bar onto this carpet. Up to then no deals over that amount were even thought of, but when the fabulous earnings of *The Birth of a Nation* became known, figures like sixty and even ninety "grand" began to be tossed around by newcomers who floated on that magic carpet, dreaming of success. Of course, there were many more flops than successes. You can boost a picture to the skies, but unless the public thinks it's good, you can't even give away tickets.

But if the picture has what it takes, the lines begin to form as if by magic. Well, I started out with a company that handled magic products, called the Magic Introduction Company. That's where my story begins.

G. W. Bitzer

March 1944

ONE

The Magic Introduction Company
1894

The first motion-picture actors came out of Union Square. Some of them were drifters who could handle props or pack films or sweep floors; most of them were young and strong, though sometimes lazy and lacking in professional skill. Others were servant girls or waitresses from the neighborhood, who could easily be seduced into appearing before the camera. Sometimes we were lucky enough to get actors from the legitimate stage who had gone broke on the road, like Griffith himself.

My entrance into the world of camerawork was like that of the actors, and it started near Union Square too. I was born in Roxbury, Massachusetts, in 1872, but it wasn't until 1894 that the urge to make something of Billy Bitzer seized me. Until then I had been satisfied with my lot as a silversmith, like my relatives and members of my family. Among other places, I had worked at Gorham's making an average of

7

twenty-five dollars a week, which was excellent pay in those days. Then I read an article that promised a great future to young men in "electrical engineering," so I enrolled in the evening courses at Cooper Union Institute, New York, where I made friends with a fellow student, Fred Loring.

Fred was employed by the Magic Introduction Company, located in the Hackett-Carhart building at 841 Broadway, on the west side of the avenue between Thirteenth and Fourteenth Streets, near Union Square. He was going west as soon as he finished his studies, and took me to meet his boss, Elias Bernard Koopman, who persuaded me to take over Fred's job. Koopman offered me twelve dollars a week, more to come later if I showed promise. I accepted less than I had been earning because I was single, twenty-two, and the work fascinated me. I had always been fascinated by magic. Whenever my sister Anna would cooperate with me, I tried every magic trick I could conjure up, with some success. Anna was three years older and always fat, and once I took her up on the roof of our home and made pictures of her seeming to walk a tightrope—my first bit of trick photography.

The Magic Introduction Company dealt in all sorts of new inventions—like a new cigar lighter that burned benzoin, and the Porter Air Lighter, which applied a chemical substance to gas jets that prevented yokels from blowing out the flames [instead of turning off the gas] and unwittingly killing themselves. This was taken up by all the leading hotels as a protection for their guests.

After I had been there several months, another novelty with magic qualities was introduced—the motion-picture camera. Its sponsor was William Kennedy Laurie Dickson, and he called his camera the Mutoscope. W. K. L. Dickson had brought his knowledge with him from the Edison Laboratory, where he had worked with the inventor on the magic box. Dickson had formed The K.M.C.D. Association with Koopman, Henry Marvin, and Herman Casler, and he had built his own brand of movie camera (Edison's was patented) with the help of the mechanics and electricians working for the Marvin and Casler rock-drill company at Canastota, New York. This camera was transported to the sixth floor at 841 Broadway, and the Magic Introduction Company became American Mutoscope in December 1895.

The first pictures we took were of loom-weaving materials which the traveling salesman could use to show merchants what they were buying. We also photographed very large machines, whose working parts could be demonstrated by this method better than they could by chart. All the salesman needed was to carry a lightweight box with a cord to hook into an electric plug. Inside the box was a series of postcard-size flip pictures, which could be stopped at any point for discussion or inspection, and were a great boon to sales.

Soon we began to make flip cards to amuse the public, as Edison had already been doing for the peep-show machines in the penny arcades. Our masterpiece, "Little Egypt," featured the most popular dancer of the day, who had come into prominence at the Chicago World's Fair. Dressed in a Turkish outfit, she swayed in a belly dance, and from her waist was suspended a tasseled ornament made of a bunch of cords. "Little Egypt," which created a great deal of excitement, was our first Mutoscope success. It was later followed by "Serpentine Dancers," "How Girls Go to Bed," "How Girls Undress," and similar tidbits. We had to build strong iron machines so that they could not be broken into and the flip cards stolen. It was really the puritanical American mind that made these pictures seem more pornographic than they were. Such pictures would be laughed at today, for the skirts were long and nudity was unknown. The nearest we got to the latter was a Mutoscope called "The Birth of the Pearl," showing a girl in white tights and bare arms crouching in an oversized oyster shell.

The Mutoscopes were followed by a period of trial and error, before movies were ready to be projected upon the screen. When this was accomplished, the company advertised that they had in their employ a staff of skilled motion-picture photographers. I was one of the staff photographers referred to in the ad. My new title marked a first step forward for me and included a raise of five dollars a week, with a promise of more to come when profit added to the invested stock. Young and high-spirited, I gave it the old soft-shoe—a-one, a-two, a-three—and I grew a mustache just like the ones that my boss, Mr. Koopman, and my idol, Mr. Dickson, had. Incidentally, I don't think W. K. L. Dickson has ever had the credit he deserves as the world's first movie cameraman. He was the granddad of us all. He started experimenting on movies for Edison as early as 1888 and photographed all the first Edison films, including "Fred Ott's Sneeze," which most people forget was a *close-up*. Later he traveled around Europe; he made the first film of Pope Leo XIII, photographed the Boer War and, according to Terry Ramsaye, he wrote the first book about movies.

---*⟨ TWO ⟩*·--

The First Presidential Film
1896

The first newsreel, or documentary, we made was of William McKinley receiving notification of his nomination to the Presidency. To get this picture, Mr. Dickson and I went to the McKinley home in Canton, Ohio. The Republican convention had already taken place that summer, and these scenes, taken in September 1896, were a re-enactment of the notification for the benefit of the people who wished to see the new Republican nominee. I was too young then to realize it was also good campaign publicity. The nominee's brother, Abner McKinley, was a stockholder in the Biograph company, as were former President Benjamin Harrison, Oscar Hammerstein, and Colonel Soper of the Pintsh Gas Company. They greatly feared the radical free-silver ideas of the Democratic nominee, William Jennings Bryan.

Mr. Dickson and I stationed ourselves upon the right side of the McKinley house, the side where it shaped out in an ell.

There the sun shone brightly, making it ideal for photographic purposes.

Mrs. McKinley was seated on the porch, in a corner, as the President came out with his secretary, George B. Cortelyou, who handed him the notification papers. The President looked them over, then took off his hat and wiped his brow with a large white handkerchief. That was all—not much, but it was what the public wanted: a picture that would go down to posterity as the first action picture of a President.

Mrs. McKinley had been on the porch, but after it was over, I noticed she had disappeared. She could not have left by herself since she was an invalid. President McKinley was most considerate of her affliction, and few people knew she was imprisoned in a wheelchair due to a nervous ailment.

We were invited inside the house for luncheon, where once more Mrs. McKinley presided. She chatted a bit, but not much. I myself had little or nothing to say, as I was merely the man who assisted Mr. Dickson, to whom I looked for instructions. Many took him for my father, especially since I had grown the mustache, emphasizing (I hoped) a resemblance. He was a magnificent dashing figure of a man, with an eye for the ladies and a manner I admired and hoped someday to achieve.

These motion pictures came out so splendidly, and the President and his party were so pleased, that we were invited to return with our camera to photograph the Inauguration parade going down F Street from the Capitol to the White House.

An Inaugural parade is a popular spectacle, and this one was a unique success because this capricious day in March ceased to bluster and we had the purest azure skies. Other Presidents had to face cold and rain, but not McKinley, the favored one.

It was two-thirty when President McKinley emerged from the basement of the Senate wing of the Capitol, arm in arm with former President Cleveland. They were followed by Senators Sherman and Mitchell, dressed in frock coats and silk hats. In the carriage on the way to the White House, President-elect McKinley sat on the right and the outgoing Cleveland on the left. Facing them sat Sherman and Mitchell. The carriage was surrounded by ten detectives who walked close by its side all the way, and they also accompanied the President to the grandstand. The police cleared our way, for Dickson and I were safe and snug in a police van which had been furnished us as a special honor, as part of the President's party.

When the day's work was done, I was both dirty and happy. I thought it a great day until I learned we had been invited to the Inaugural dinner held at the Ebbett House. Mr. Dickson was all primed for the occasion, having brought along a dress suit, but I had only the clothes on my back. Naturally I tried to get out of going, but Mr. Dickson insisted. He gave me a clean shirt and tie, and told me to get a shave and come out smiling.

I was young and bashful and green in social graces, though I had attended German socials and affairs at the club my father belonged to in Boston. On entering the dining room we found the table beautifully set with silver and shining glass. The fern decorations and the clean white linen made me wish my sister Anna was there to see it. I got through the evening somehow or other.

Our first public showing of motion pictures was given at the Olympia, an Oscar Hammerstein theater, on the evening of October 12, 1896. While the photographing itself had been fairly easy and gratifying, the showing of these pictures was anything but. I learned from Mr. Koopman that this was to be my responsibility; no one else wanted to take it on.

Running the projector was like running a trolley car, in that it made a terrible racket. The projector was also hand-turned, like the camera. I used every resource I had, including my nose, to control the film so that it would not buckle on me. I was scared stiff and almost desperate when I realized that I would have so many different things to do—flashing titles onto the screen with a separate lantern-slide projector; watching the heat from the lamp so there would be no danger of fire; looking at the screen to keep the action smooth; and so on. I would have to use both hands, one foot, my forehead, and my nose; and I was afraid that two eyes would not be enough.

Much secrecy surrounded everything we did, both with the camera and with the projectors, and though nothing was ever said, I knew that in back of it all was fear of legal action by the Edison interests. At 841 Broadway we had a large darkroom for developing our film, a smaller room to print the film, and an even smaller room used as an experimental workshop. As I recollect, when we got to breaking in the men who were to operate the Biograph projectors, I connected the house current to the knob on the outside door, with an insulated plate holding it, so that any inquisitive new man would get a shock if curiosity prompted him to pry around when, as sometimes happened, I rushed out without locking the door. But after I got some shocks myself, I cut this out.

The showing at the Olympia was the first time I would have to run the projector away from our workrooms at 841 Broadway. The projector was an enormous seven-foot-tall, upright affair, resembling a coffin, especially when standing on its end in one of the mid-balcony boxes at the Olympia which had been converted into a makeshift "projection booth." At the press preview, the reporters sat in the gallery on the next level above the projector. Running this thrasher for a handful of reporters seemed little different to me from running it in the loft farther down Broadway.

When the press screening started, the first thing that struck me was that I had the picture a little high on the screen. I had the coffin very slightly tipped forward, with a piece of wood under it. I was afraid to tip it further, lest its vibration topple it over into the orchestra seats below. There wasn't much space for bracing it anyway. I had the little magic lantern (stereopticon) which projected the title slides placed in front of the projector lower down at the side. On the floor there were also a couple of large, bulky rheostats, to control the flow of electric current, with their wires lying about. I had glass slides in my jacket pocket and had to keep shifting them from my right pocket to my left, as the shown slides were pretty hot. An electric switch was also on the floor, because I had no place to put it without mutilating the booth. I had hung some maroon-colored drapes on either side of the railing in front of the booth to prevent the balcony occupants on either side from peeking in. In addition, there were a couple of fire pails filled with sand, the box I brought the film down in, a stack of tools, and a wood saw!

The *modus operandi* was this: the full reel of film was evenly adjusted upon the large upper brass pulley, its diameter being about ten inches, with its eight or ten pictures across its diameter. After adjusting the reel upon the pulley, I kept it covered with a couple of damp towels, since it was not advisable to thread the machine completely until you were about ready to run. There was a long stretch between the reel and where it came to the first set of pulleys, and if left too long in the air, the film would curl up like a hose. Just before the finish of the vaudeville act onstage, ahead of the Biograph, I threaded the film over the wooden pulleys, clamped the webbed driving-belt as the film made the long lower loop, two feet long, leading it over another series of rollers, and gripping it on to the take-up pulley. Then I threw on the main switch, turned on a smaller switch, and put the first slide into position. It was the American Biograph trademark, a spreading eagle. The show was finally under way.

In the Biograph lamp, which was also a 25-amp Colt hand-feed lamp with gimping down to the front lamp, I put on the next slide, then stepped back up to the big upright coffin. There was a single step up into this booth, which raised the rear chairs higher. I gingerly started the large motor controller, my left hand reaching up to help guide the film. When it got up to speed, my right hand quickly clutched the rod that controlled the picture on the screen. The beater cam movement, which pulled the picture down into position, was uneven and could gain or lose in the aperture frame. The lever which operated a friction drive disk controlled this; when I put my foot down and pushed, the pedal would open the light gate.

I had hung a mirror in a wooden frame on the front drape, at an angle which enabled me to intermittently observe how the film was feeding. If it tried to creep toward the edge of the feeder pulley, I would give it a push back with my forehead or nose. I straightened it out enough to finish the first one-minute picture, all the while keeping my eyes pretty well glued to the screen, otherwise the picture would have started riding up and down. There was a slack leader between pictures, and bang! off went the motor control.

With a jump at the big reel on top, I had to stop its momentum when the reel was full. As the film piled up on the take-up reel, I slapped a monkey wrench onto one of its spokes to help it hold the film as the diameter increased. Then I pulled the next slide out of my pocket and went down to the slide lantern, which rested on a board with one end on a chair and the other on the balcony rail.

After this press preview, I began to wonder how I could tilt the machine. As I said before, the picture was a bit too high on the screen. I couldn't tip the coffin much, because the top would hit the ceiling. There wasn't any mechanism right near the box, so I took the wood saw and cut into the overhang, a center partition piece included. Then on the coffin's projecting feet I nailed a couple of wooden braces, which extended forward down to the corner of the floor and balcony rail. This really made the coffin steadier, but apparently I had also knocked the whole clumsy but delicate mechanism out of alignment. It simply would not run without buckling when I tried it out after sawing off the top. After repeated adjustments in which I followed all suggestions, even those of Henry Marvin, nothing helped.

The dog film, which I used for testing purposes, would run one time but not the next. I finally said, "Let me alone and I will have it ready and running in time for the show."

We had a fellow, Jack Miller by name, who got his job with Mutoscope as a sort of contact man, a location-getter we would call them today. He was a real Mr. Know-it-all, who kept breathing down my neck until Mr. Marvin finally pulled him away, saying, "Let Bitzer alone. He'll fix it all right."

"If it fails tonight," Miller scornfully threatened, "Hammerstein will throw you right out the window, down onto Broadway."

Then he locked me in the booth. Imagine, two powerful open arc lamps, a hunk of nitroglycerine big as a roll of garden hose, flimsy cotton-nap curtains, and me—alone. There wasn't room for another man anyway, and he couldn't have helped a bit if there had been room. When I look back to that memorable night, I think the operators' union would have given me a Gold Card, for merit over and above the call of duty. (I later received a cameraman's union Gold Card for much less.) However, in 1896 there was no such union.

The show went off fine, thank God. When the last picture, of the Empire State Express, ended, it was followed by applause and cheers. Then there was stamping and pounding on the booth door, and I nearly collapsed. I thought the whole back of the machine had blown up, or at least fallen off, such was my nervous tension. This had been my first running of a public show.

If you wonder why there was so much unpreparedness at this first Biograph showing, it may have been because—as I understood it when I first worked for the American Mutoscope Company—their patents allowed them to make only peep-show machines. But after Edison's Vitascope screening at Koster & Bial's Music Hall on April 20, 1896, American Mutoscope was determined to reach the screen with its Biograph films as quickly as possible.

Up in Canastota, they began furiously building the mechanism for a projector. We had made several experiments, in which we threw the two arc lights on the Mutoscope (opaque) bromide-paper pictures as they revolved on the reel. We projected them with this reflected light, panopticon method, but they paled into insignificance in comparison to the brilliant image given by the transparent film lighted directly. We took a few parts out of our first bulky camera mechanism; they had interfered with the incorporation of a mirror into which, at right angles, we shot the rays of an arc light. We also pulled the teeth of the camera (that is, the punches which perforated sprocket holes in the film during picture taking). The effect with this wide film was magnificent. Together with our thirty pictures per second, compared to the other's sixteen per second, we had an obviously superior product in the Biograph method.

The projector was shipped to New York and assembled on the sixth floor of 841 Broadway. To me it was more like the Wright Brothers' first flying machine than a projector. The skeleton framework of wooden two-by-fours reached seven feet up from the floor. The braces ran out at an angle from the top of the frame to the floor, and there were additional projecting pieces to hold the arc lamp. We stuck to shooting the lamp's ray into a mirror, which in turn reflected the beam of light through the film. We were a bit timid about having this open arc light in between the celluloid and having the film run over or under it. So it was put out on the side.

The mirror itself was made of copperplates, about four inches square; and we not only had it silver-plated but also hand-polished and burnished to secure a perfectly flat surface. I took the copperplates to Gorham's and had some of my old cronies, as well as relatives, mystified when I gave them our specifications. They made what I wanted at considerable expense, and it came out perfectly, with no distortion. An ordinary mirror glass would have given a double reflection and might have cracked with the heat.

After this freaky-looking Biograph projector, with its

wheels, pulleys, friction discs, and all the rest, was ready, Hammerstein himself would bring down a group and we would run the machine for them. It was enclosed in canvas-duck curtains. I would wrap these curtains around the entire piece of machinery every night, using ropes and sealing the tie knots with my initial, so that no one could look at the machine during the night without my knowledge.

Since I was the only operator, every time the film would run off the pulleys, rip, or tear, I was blamed—by Mr. Koopman especially. "What did you do to it now? It was running all right. Leave it alone or get out," he would say. After the others had gone, he would look for me out on the sixth-floor fire escape, where I went to cool off and calm down, and ask me simply what I thought had caused it to buckle. These were all the projector "previews" we ever had on the sixth floor, until Herman Casler sent down the new projector I have described as a "coffin."

In the winter of 1895, it was the American Mutoscope Company. In 1899 it became the American Mutoscope *and* Biograph Company. It was not until the spring of 1909 that we finally were called the Biograph. In 1899, the next camera built for Biograph by the Marvin and Casler shop at Canastota was really a de luxe streamliner. You may wonder why this first Biograph camera was built so bulky and correspondingly heavy, compared to the Edison motion-picture cameras in use at that date. The latter were more of a shoebox size, with their smaller bands of film perforated with cute little sprocket holes along the sides, running over watchlike star wheels (sprockets). This Edison film was one inch wide, while Mutoscope and Biograph made their film some nine times larger in area, or $2\frac{23}{32}$

inches wide. We had no sprocket holes along the sides, which made it necessary for our film to be run by friction. Our machine also perforated two holes, one on either side of each exposure, at the instant of exposing the sensitized surface to light. They were master holes, guides for the printing of the positive, which would steady the film for projection purposes, as our friction system was anything but steady.

We also had an air pump, which operated during the taking of a picture to hold the film flat against the aperture frame; a blower, too, to expel the perforations cut out by the punches; and finally a heating device to prevent static.

Even after the Biograph had reduced its film from the wide size to the postage-stamp-size standard film, they were still compelled, because of patent legislation and the pressures of the Motion Picture Patents Company, to stick to this beater cam pull-down movement and friction-driven film idea—until the time, much later, when they also became part of the Motion Picture Patents Company. For our Mutoscope peep shows, we perfected a scheme to assemble and hold the one thousand bromide paper pictures, with card backing to stiffen them. Herman Casler was the brain department for this sort of thing up in Canastota. Mutoscope reels were like taking a stack of playing cards and mounting them upright, on and over a round wood block. The first ones were hand-assembled, and it was a Chinese puzzle to squeeze and crowd, say, the last pack of cards around the block and have them all—from one to 999—steady. With each backing card, they bulked some two thousand cards.

We wore elastic armbands to keep our sleeves up in those days, some of which had cotton/silk webbing covering. We got the idea that by punching a round hole through the cards, putting an opened sleeve elastic through the holes, and fastening the rubber together again, this would hold cards in a circle. It could be stretched over the huge wooden spool, and metal flanges would help to clinch the cards on the sides.

I was sent out to find a place where such flanges might be made. I went down to Centre Street and saw a sign: MASON AND RAUSCH, EXPERT MACHINISTS AND MODEL MAKERS, ONE FLIGHT UP. Here I explained what I wanted as a sort of set of wheels to hold some cards in place. I didn't want to reveal too much as it was all very hush-hush at the time.

In pioneering, where one does not know more than another, mishaps occur, and I sure made my share of mistakes: fogged film, mechanisms jamming, buckled film, a storage battery not working. Imperfections we just called static scratches or underexposed film. No matter what you called them, the man behind the gun got the blame, especially if he was not a good alibi artist. I was the Mr. Milquetoast type, and I was sure that if several mishaps happened, I would be fired.

We had no union for recourse, but like Bumpstead I got used to the routine. I recollect at least a dozen times when I turned in my keys, took my belongings from the studio, and with bowed head and heavy heart left Biograph forever. Some of the causes were thoughtless and unjust. Like the time when after much experimenting to prevent static marks, I hit on the idea of heating the inside of the camera with a *bicycle lamp burning alcohol*. It worked well indoors, but the first real cold day steamed up the inside of the lens so that it may as well have been a ground-glass surface I was shooting through. The whole day's work was lost, and with it my job.

Later they sent for me with an admonition aimed at the humble man who likes his job and wants to keep it: "If you promise to keep your mind on your work, we'll give you your camera back. Stop playing around with the office money. It comes out of your pay next time." You just don't fool around with a possible pay cut, so I'd keep my nose to the grindstone until another day when I'd forget and try out another new idea I hoped would work.

As many times as I was "fired," I always went back to Biograph, once even after I had agreed to take a job at another studio. And each time they would come forth with more money, not much, but enough to top what I would be getting elsewhere. For this reason I was always just a little ahead, salary-wise, of other cameramen in the two or three companies then working in New York.

We never worked with contracts. It was always just our mutual consent and respect—a gentleman's agreement. Today the cameraman gets his setup on a big scene already laid out, places his various cameramen at such angles as are dictated. If, say, a close-up shot is desired, he turns his lens turret with its variety of focal length lenses (even telephoto). Or one of the surrounding cameramen might be getting a closer angle and a better shot. So there you are.

Such a cameraman never has the fun I had of jumping hither and yon with my camera to take long shots of trenches, or shots of one group, then another, or of the principals behind the second group, then a close shot of a big hand clasping a locket, or back and forth on the battlefield, then shots of a man's face begrimed with powder, smoke, and sweat—all in a series of maneuvers with the same camera. There was satisfaction in having put in a good day's work, and in waiting for the laboratory men's word of approval. The end of each day only meant, "What are we shooting tomorrow?"

⸺⊰ THREE ⊱⸺

Nora

Biograph built a studio on the roof of the building at 841 Broadway. The sixth floor, where we had offices, was the top floor, and one flight up was the roof. The booth for the camera was sealed tight against light, or the elements, with black tar paper. The stage, however, had to be open to the sunlight, which for several years remained our chief source of light for taking pictures. Mr. Koopman had already gone to England to sell the Biograph products in London.

The New York Central appreciated the advertising value of the movie we had taken of the Empire State Express. Our picture-taking equipment, which was very heavy and cumbersome, as I shall always remember, was transported over their lines free of charge. The camera operators received courtesy-free passage anywhere they wished to go. We were invited to avail ourselves of special engines, or cars, for the purpose of taking movies of the scenery along the way.

This led to other railroads making similar offers. The advertising was then put on a commercial basis—first by the Union Pacific, whose crack train, the Overland Limited, we photographed. Most of the engines on the Union Pacific were wood burners, with that funny inverted funnel-shaped stack and cow-fender.

Next came the Canadian Pacific, contracting with us for movies. I started on one trip for them which covered thirty thousand miles from the time I started until I returned, about two months. On these combined railroads, my trip took me from New York to California, photographing the New York Central, Michigan Central, Chicago Northwestern, Union Pacific, and on lines from Montreal to Nova Scotia. During this time I was always supplied with my own special car. Franking privileges on the telegraph division and Pullman service were also included. I could go anywhere I wished at any time. I lived practically all the time in the private car hooked on to the end of the train, with an adequate wide platform to operate from.

Between traveling on trains and living alone in furnished rooms, I got to learn a lot about life and women. I knew now what the hotel clerk meant when he asked, "A room with, or without?" but I hadn't known the first time. The Harvey House waitresses were more to my liking than all the sporting women in the world. You could trust them. They were workers like myself, and I was at ease with them.

It was just about the end of our run at the junction yard in New Jersey, and we were awaiting word from headquarters as to our next move. Charlie Greer was traveling with me at this point. The night was nasty, cold, and bleak, and no one was around at the junction yard, just Greer and myself. It was so cold that we walked the tracks rather than stand and shiver. We hadn't gone far when we saw a bright light in the sky, silhouetting a building which we knew to be the Junction Hotel. Suddenly we realized it was on fire. We hastened toward it and could now see it was the building next to the hotel; this was the servants' quarters. Someone yelled there were still a couple of women up there, the cook and her assistant, so Charlie and I decided to get them out, like in the movies. We ran up, and opening the first door, we found the two women slumped over on the floor. Charlie and I grabbed blankets, and each of us tossed an unconscious woman over his back like a sack and fled downstairs.

Out in the street we turned them over to the waiting ambulance without seeing their faces and waited around until the fire was extinguished before we went back to the train.

Nothing more to do now but turn in. Charlie took the whole thing calmly. I was excited and would have loved discussing it, but I didn't want to appear naïve. Charlie was different, he was a married man. The smell of smoke from the burning building was still clinging to our clothing. I closed my eyes and saw myself as a hero who had just had a daring adventure. Then I wondered how much of my experience could be used later when we did a rescue scene at the studio.

Next morning was clear and not so cold, and there was still no word from the office, but there was word from the women we had rescued. It came in the form of a little old priest who said the women wanted to thank the two fine gentlemen kindly for saving their lives the night before. I asked Charlie Greer if he wanted to go, but he said he didn't.

Arriving at the hospital, the priest and I went at once to the bedsides. Instinctively I knew which woman was mine, for I had had a glimpse of her ginger-brown hair. The other woman appeared older. Mine was sort of cute and had a brogue nearly as thick as the priest's. I don't remember what was said, but I do remember she had little blue ribbons in her hair which matched her eyes. As I looked at her, I experienced a foolish and unrestrainable urge to take her in my arms. Instead I gave Nora Farrell my card and asked her to come see me if ever she was in New York.

Soon I was back at 841 Broadway, fulfilling my job as troubleshooter. Among my other duties was one which no cameraman today would consider part of his job. When a machine was installed in a theater by us, we gave a guarantee that if anything went amiss, we would correct it at once or give them a refund. Most complaints were of unruly projection machines which perhaps had a tendency to rip the film or become jerky. I also acted as house electrician; my course at Cooper Union entitled me to that license. Perhaps my first lesson started me off right. A projection machine installed in a store on the Bowery had suddenly ceased to function. The projector had not been installed by me, and whoever did the job located a switch, or main, on which to hook his wire. When the machine was turned on, lo and behold, the arc light burned out. The owner gave up on it and asked for the troubleshooter—me.

Arriving at the scene with my kit of tools, I followed the wires in the building and came to a dark hole underneath the sidewalk where the wiring suddenly ceased. "Better be careful going in there, young man," the janitor behind me warned in a voice of caution. Like the village constable showing his shield, I had the confidence that goes with the novice.

"That's all right, I know, I know," I assured him. As I stepped forward to reach for the switch, a loose wire I had not noticed came in contact with my forehead. I was thrown backward some ten feet by a high polarity wire of different voltage. It was an alternating current which was fed from the sidewalk lamp outside the store. Covered with debris, I had to crawl out and begin all over again, but this time I listened to the advice of the janitor.

On the roof studio we were making pictures that ran on an average of seventy-five feet apiece. There was no story. The set consisted of two large Japanese screens spread to make a background, a table, and a few chairs. If it was a domestic scene, I put paper roses in a vase on the center of the table. If it was a home of wealth, the table was removed and a large potted palm was placed by the Japanese screen. Two potted palms indicated even greater wealth. Having no actors, we would just take anyone handy. According to the number of people we could gather together, the plot was born.

The Interrupted Message was my first staged attempt at a movie (I had taken only newsreels and railroad "scenics"). For the new venture, director, cameraman, props, and writer were all rolled up in one Billy Bitzer. We used a couple of women from the building for the feminine lure and a man from the lobby bar for the comedy bit. This was a domestic scene, and I placed the women on the left and right of the table. The man was relating an experience, with many gestures, when there was a knock on the door. The two women were giving rapt attention to his discourse, as they rocked back and forth in their chairs. It was up to the man telling the story to answer the door, but he must also finish his story. He opens the door, accepts the letter, puts it on the table, but continues his rapid talking as he seats himself. He reaches to the floor to retrieve his handkerchief, but instead picks up the end of the tablecloth, which he sticks in his pocket. (On the end of the tablecloth we had a hook.) At last he reads the message. On it I had written: "You're a lousy actor." He hadn't expected this, looked around helplessly in astonishment, then jumped to his feet, dashing from the room. As he dashed out, the hook in his pocket pulled off the tablecloth, thereby upsetting one of the women. This was the effect we wanted, as petticoats were amazingly attractive in an era when ladies dressed to suggest rather than reveal. (A hint of lace or ruffles on a petticoat was daring and titillating; the mere sight of lace was a wondrous thing, a real eyepopper, and we pursued that line of thought for our penny-arcade and early pictures.) Such was *The Interrupted Message*.

We also learned early that children are scene-stealers. *Hard Wash* was a comedy and a big laugh-getter, but strictly for the screen. We used a young colored mother and her little Jo-Jo, a cute and very black child. He was getting a bath. His back was to the camera as he stood in a basin of water on the kitchen table. Mommy had a large sponge full of white soap suds and a big bar of soap. She started lathering his arms, shoulders, legs, and backside, covering him with great quantities of the white soapy foam. On top of his head she made a mountainous lather, which she drew to a peak. Then she wet the sponge in the basin, held it over his head for a showerlike rinse that sent the foamy white suds running down his black shoulders and stomach, then turned him profile so it spouted off his little peter. It went over big in the nickelodeons.

I Want My Dinner! was another child picture. Ross Mc-

Cutcheon, the three-year-old son of Wally, our director-in-chief, was a husky redhead, the youthful counterpart of Spencer Tracy. Chubby and rosy-cheeked, he was a natural battler, and how he loved to eat! He went after food with such zest that we thought it might make a good movie. We starved him all morning, and he was as rebellious as any young animal would be. He fretted and cried, and as time and his appetite grew, his cries became deafening. "I want my oatmeal!" he demanded. When it had gone as far as his mother would allow, we put him in a highchair, where we had to strap him down. While he was still fighting and howling, I started to grind. The audience could see only a hand putting the bowl of food before him on the highchair tray. He pounced upon that dish of food with spoon and fist, emptying it quickly, getting large quantities of mush over his face and down the front of his clothes. When the bowl was empty and he was satisfied there was no more there, he turned on his hands and face, licking himself as far as his tongue would go. Then he broke out in a large infectious grin of complete satisfaction. The picture not only traveled around the world with great success, but Kaiser Wilhelm even sent Ross a silver cup and a letter commending him on his wonderful performance.

"A young lady to see you, Mr. Bitzer," Joe, the office boy, phoned up to the roof studio. "She's waiting downstairs."

"Tell her to wait right there, I'll be down." I was sure it would be Nora. I rushed right down to greet her, but I hadn't expected she would be so small: I couldn't believe this tiny woman was the heavy bundle I had pitched over my back the night of the fire. Holding on to her arm, I said, "I've been thinking about you a lot, and I'm so glad you're here at last."

I noticed everything about her: her tiny hands and feet, blue eyes, white skin, and ginger-brown hair. She had an appeal for me that made me very happy.

We walked through Thirteenth Street, east from Broadway, avoiding the congested shopping area of Fourteenth Street. The barrel smell from open basements and the odor from horse-drawn wagons on the wet cobblestone—that was the city smell in those days. I hoped the contrast would greatly enhance the aroma of good wholesome German cooking. I loved to show off, especially with girls. Besides, Nora was a professional cook, so I felt the need to impress her with my culinary savoir-faire.

As we came through the rear entrance of Luchow's new and popular restaurant, a waiter motioned for our choice of booth or open table. Ordinarily I would have preferred a booth. Nora indicated her preference by walking over to a table by the street window, so I followed along after her.

We sipped our cold golden beer, smiling more than talking. I took a hot roll from the basket, broke this in half, and offered it to Nora. She accepted. Her expression altered as she looked into my eyes. "Yes?" she spoke softly, leading me on. We spent the rest of the meal flirting and teasing. It was all very pleasant and I had no desire to end our little feast and go back to work, but I must. We made a date for the following Sunday. I was to call for her at her sister's place in the Bronx and meet the Redford family.

Sunday morning I had to be at work splicing my "News Happenings" film. I finished about noon, walked back to my furnished room, and changed to clean clothes.

I arrived at the Redford flat in the midst of a family row. Nora was storming through the flat, fighting with her sister and brother-in-law, as well as with an Irish policeman named Joe Leary, who, it seems, had been her boy friend until she met me. The family was demanding she leave at once and never darken their door again. There was much throwing of garments from one side of the room to the other. Finally, we found ourselves forced out together into the hall, with me picking up the articles as they threw them out and Nora beating in defiance on the door, which had suddenly been locked against our re-entry. I straightened out her clothes, and together we walked quietly over to the elevated train. She clung to me like a kitten, begging me to protect her.

In the family fight, a lot had been revealed to me about Nora, but she appealed to me even though she was older by ten years than I. When you are in your twenties, ten years don't seem much, but later they did. I wanted her for myself, though I later found her to be as unpredictable as a detour sign. We boarded the Jerome line, which took us down to Fourteenth Street, where I smuggled her up to my room. After that night, we saw each other every time I was in town. As time went on, she knew where to find me any hour of the day or night, same as my boss. Maybe she was just one of the charming Irish I admired. I had saved her life, and this made our relationship special. To me she was a welcome and lovable obligation.

--◦⊰ FOUR ⊱◦--

Filming My First War
1898

Spain, Spain, Spain,
You oughta be ashame'
For blowing up the battleship THE MAINE.

The Biograph movie camera was out after scoops called
"News Happenings," when word came that the U.S. Navy
battleship *Maine* had been blown up in Havana Harbor, so I
was sent with my cumbersome camera to cover the story.

I embarked upon the *Seguranca*, reaching Havana on Feb-
ruary 19, 1898, four days after the news broke. On Wednes-
day morning we sighted in the distance old Morro Castle, a
sheer two hundred feet above the sea. To the left of Morro
was La Socaha, and ahead stretched a winding waterway bor-
dered by palm-fringed shores. At the entrance to the bay we
passed Estrella Point and Cayo Smith, a picturesque, hilly is-
let. It was then we came abreast of the battleship *Maine*, an

33

unrecognizable mass of scrap iron, twisted and mangled. Only a single hulk remained, from which flew the American flag, in what appeared defiance of those who had destroyed her.

Visiting Cuba under Spanish rule was highly dangerous. With bag and baggage we were hustled into the Customs House. My camera was bulky enough, but when you consider it was driven by a motor operated by over two thousand pounds of storage batteries, packed in many boxes, which the officials insisted on examining, all this took much time. The grins and leers on the faces of the bystanders gave me to understand this was unfriendly territory. Luckily I had been warned beforehand to go straight to the Ingleterra Hotel, where I would find comfort and safety. As I learned later, it was well for me that I was one to follow orders. After checking in at the hotel, I went back to the wreckage of the *Maine* to take pictures.

Divers were at work recovering bodies—at one end Spanish divers, and at the other Americans. I knew it would be impossible for me, with my bulky camera, to get pictures that would tell the true story, but our boys with still cameras did such admirable work that today in the photo section of the Library of Congress you are able to see it for yourself. All I got was moving pictures of the *Maine* as seen from the shore.

I remained in Havana, trying to get pictures from a towboat, and then we were ordered back to New York on the same day Ambassador Fitzhugh Lee evacuated Havana. In New York they kept me busy on "News Happenings," and it was not until April 21 (my twenty-sixth birthday, incidentally) that I returned, as war was then declared by the United States.

I happened to be in Boston covering more news when the

Biograph office telegraphed that arrangements had been made with the New York *Journal* for several newsmen, two still photographers, and myself with the movie outfit to go aboard a towboat to cover the war in Cuba. This time my journey took me to Siboney, the point where our battleships had cleared out the Spanish to make a landing for our troops. I took some shots of the troops landing from the "Yale" and "Harvard" transports, and other shots along the beach.

I found myself helpless to advance with the troops because of the scarcity of horses. Horses had been shipped all right, but most of them had drowned. The horses had simply been pushed overboard without anyone holding up their heads, and the weight of a horse in rough water was too much. They had drowned because no one there knew how to handle the situation before it got out of hand. Those in charge of the landing had been greatly at fault.

Without means of transportation to follow the troops, I returned to my towboat, where we stationed ourselves, taking pictures each morning as the battleships in Havana harbor fired on the sand batteries about Morro Castle. Through binoculars we could see the clouds of sand and what seemed to be bodies of men and fragments of guns flying in the air toward us. At this point we were ordered out to sea, with threats of arrest if we came in line of the battleship fire again. We stationed ourselves three miles out, in international waters, awaiting a reprieve. I was relieved by this, remembering a near-miss shell that struck the water just a little in front of us and ricocheted over my head. I had pulled the focusing cloth I was using just a little further over my head, like a damn fool, but continued grinding out the action nevertheless.

We remained on the towboat waiting for the big naval battle that was rumored. We were growing impatient when one morning a crew man shook me awake: "Your big boss is outside, it's time to get up." Then I saw the yacht *Sylvia* standing across the water, so we were taken over to her. Aboard was William Randolph Hearst of the New York *Journal*, accompanied by Jack Follansbee, James Creelman, and two pretty young ladies who were sisters. It looked mighty inviting after all the tedious hours we had spent. Here were champagne and lively companionship. One still-cameraman of our party needed ice in developing his plates, and here we had plenty of ice. This change from the smell of tar rope and oil and the confined quarters of the towboat was the best remedy we could have to relieve tension and refresh our spirits.

The *Sylvia* had just arrived that morning, and they were all anxious to go sightseeing. This would be difficult if the girls were seen by the sailors on the battleships, so to prevent this, the girls donned male attire. We were in the delirious state of being under fire in war time, and we got more friendly than we would have at home; the crew mixed with the guests and vice versa. Having discovered that the Spanish fleet was lying at anchor in Havana harbor, our fleet, the North American Squadron, promptly bottled their exit by sinking the *Merrimac* across the entrance of the harbor. I could not get pictures, as this took place at night.

I decided at this juncture to land with my Frankenstein-like camera and exert new efforts to obtain battle scenes. Frederic Remington, who was returning to the States, gave me his horse to view the prospects and pull the camera ashore. Then I was ready to follow the troops inland. The outposts were within a few miles of Havana, so I started with my camera toward General William R. Shafter's headquarters, halfway between my starting point and the front line.

I took movies of the general with his staff, crossing a stream on horseback. He was a portly gentleman and filled the area of the postal-card movie field so well that it was unnecessary to worry about filling in the background. Here I was again met by the Hearst party, minus the girls. Leaving my camera temporarily, I joined them as we neared the front.

We passed different companies of soldiers, some marching in stoic silence toward what perhaps to them was death. As we walked along, we heard some Gatling gunfire. I still hadn't seen the Cuban outpost. Just to the right were the Roosevelt Rough Riders. The fighting continued. We heard the ping of a Spanish bullet, snipping away a piece of bark from a skinny palm over our heads; a few more singing bullets and then we sought cover. Straight ahead was a Spanish blockhouse which seemed deserted. I saw one of our party, Creelman, from whom I had just separated, trying to climb up to the blockhouse, carrying an American flag in his teeth. Over the blockhouse, the red and yellow Spanish flag was flying. Creelman had just reached the roof and exchanged the flags when a Spanish Mauser bullet hit him in the shoulder, knocking him down. I rushed up to him, picked him up, got him to put his good arm around my neck, and we started back. It was a slow descent. When we did reach first aid, they were able to stop the flow of blood. Slowly we wended our way from the battle, resting repeatedly. As the journey from Kettle Hill, which we were on, to Siboney was some fourteen miles and we had to walk all the way, it took us almost two days to get back. Finally, we again came to General Shafter's headquarters, where there was a doctor on hand. Creelman's wound was really attended to now, and he was supplied with ample medicine and bandages for the return to the yacht *Sylvia*.

I myself was feeling none too well as, after landing in Cuba,

I drank some water which caused me to take on a yellow complexion and suffer from dysentery. There were cases of yellow fever around and I felt I had possibly contracted it.

Back aboard the *Sylvia,* we found everything as lively as we had left it. Hearst and Follansbee had now returned, without a scratch or bruise. We got Creelman down to his bunk, and there he remained in pain from his wound and from the motion of the yacht as it rocked its way home through choppy waters.

My sickness got worse, so I kept to my bunk directly opposite Creelman's cabin. I stirred occasionally to go up on deck to get some air and much needed sunshine. The rest of the party played it safe by keeping away from us. To be sure, our food was brought and left at the door by the crew, but it was dangerous to come too close, lest they catch what I had, and we seemed to manage without them. It was only when the sisters were racing about, full of fun and laughter, that I saw or heard anyone else.

By the time the yacht sailed into Baltimore, I was a deep yellow. It was decided it would be dangerous for us to land in daylight, where I might be observed and everyone quarantined, so it was arranged we would land on the outskirts unobserved in the night and each go his separate way, meeting again in New York. My camera was to remain on board and later would be shipped to New York. All I took with me was my suitcase.

I wandered around the streets in the poor section of Baltimore, looking for a doctor. The one I found took me in at once, called his nurse, and together they worked over me, not really knowing what it was I had. He gave me a drink like malted milk and some medicine; then they took turns fanning me while I rested and slept for two hours until train time. He called a hack driver, took me to the depot, and placed me in my berth on the train, after giving me medicine to take on the journey and strict orders to go to a hospital when I arrived at the railroad terminal in Hoboken.

The night was hot, or so it seemed to me, as I placed my face against the open window screen and slept. In the morning I went into the washroom, where two men withdrew quickly as they took one look at me.

They know I have yellow fever, I thought, but on looking in the mirror, I was startled to see that the soot from the open window the night before was now on my face. Instead of washing it away and having the yellow skin show through, I rubbed the soot in to avoid detection.

I crossed to New York on the ferry, took the crosstown streetcar, and immediately sleep overcame me. At the end of the line the conductor roused me, thinking I was a bum, and told me it was the last stop.

Slowly I dragged myself to Post-Graduate Hospital, where I collapsed on the steps. Someone came out and took me in. I gave my name and turned over my money, but I dared not tell them I had come from Cuba. I was taken to a bed, where I lay more dead than alive for four days. It was typhoid malaria. When I was able to talk, I asked them to send for my sister, Anna, and for Nora. I thought I was dying and that this was the end.

As I was one of the first cases of typhoid malaria they would soon be treating in the hundreds, doctors from everywhere rushed to my aid. With all this care, I still was sick for sixteen weeks. My weight went from 165 to 97 pounds. My bones stuck out and I could not rest, for lying in bed had made my skin sore. I was never more ravenously hungry in my life than during my stay at the hospital. They couldn't give me food because of my high fever, but still I longed for it.

Nora was the first to come, her arms filled with roses and her lips warm for kissing. Never was I so happy to see anyone. We arranged then and there to take a flat; there would be no more furnished rooms. She would nurse me back to health, and we could manage with the money I had coming in back pay.

When sister Anna came shortly after, I had already set the pattern of my life, but I kept this to myself. I should have told my family about Nora, but some obstinate German stubbornness in my make-up cautioned me against it. Like all good sisters, Anna criticized my way of life, my roving occupation, and my lack of responsibility. She felt she had wasted her time since our mother died, trying to make something of me. She was busy and content with her little family, living in the 114th Street flat with her husband, John Bitzer, and son, Louis. I, with my restless ways, had gone wrong when I gave up silversmithing for my uncertain life in the movies.

I thought back to the sad Christmas in 1881 when we buried Mother, Anna Marie Schmidt. Christmas with Mother in our Roxbury, Massachusetts, house had always been joyful until then. When we returned from the sad little funeral, I trimmed the tree Father had brought home, so that my two-year-old brother, Carl, and twelve-year-old sister, Anna, would not be so sad. I recollect Father sitting in stoic silence, without really seeing, overcome by Mother's sudden demise after only three days of pneumonia. I was nine years old.

In our home near the old Walpole ballpark, outside Boston,

a silence such as we had never known descended. Father was a blacksmith by trade and worked hard making harnesses for horses and hoops for carriage wheels, beside shoeing horses and using the forge and anvil. Housekeepers came and went at our house, for they all had an eye for Father, until he decided to let sister Anna take over. She was a better housekeeper at twelve than many of them, and as time went on, she was like a mother to us, even to Father. Anna and I were given little public-school education, for it wasn't compulsory in those days. We got most of our schooling from Saturday and Sunday school (Lutheran), where there were volunteer teachers who took personal interest and pride in their pupils. As I grew old enough to qualify for work, I had a leaning toward things mechanical. Next to machinery, I liked lettering shops. After that I liked magic tricks. I learned magic from books, but much of it I learned watching magicians on the stage.

When I was about seventeen (1889), our household was upset when Anna announced she intended marrying our cousin, John Bitzer. After a lot of beefing, we settled down to the idea and gave them a grand wedding. The bride and groom left Roxbury for their new home in Providence, Rhode Island. For the next year we had housekeepers again, and I took work in a jewelry sweatshop, which paid well. I learned here that money isn't everything. They used some sort of chemical from which I developed granulated eyelids and hives. This became so severe Father decided to send me to friends of his who lived on a farm. I didn't care for farm life or wish to be a farmer, so I ran away and returned to Father. He became very upset with me and wrote to Anna in Providence, asking if she could make room for me. It was then that my brother-in-law cousin started me working with him at Gorham's, the silverware house. I enjoyed it there, and we were a warm, close-knit family.

I got interested in the Providence town sport—bicycle racing. I was girl-shy, afraid of them, although I did have a steady girl, Emma Walde; but she met and married a young chemist from St. Louis. Now all my money went toward a fine bike and I started training in earnest for the races. Monte Scott was the champion cyclist of Rhode Island, and I set out to match him as quickly as possible, for I wanted to start at the top. I joined the Rhode Island League of Wheelermen. I had one of those machines called an *ordinary*. It stood fifty-three inches high, with a large wheel in front and a small wheel in back. It took a lot of pedaling on that little wheel to make the large one go around; if you were not careful, you could pedal too hard, lose your balance, and pitch forward head over wheel. I entered several local one-mile races and won. I began to feel the thrill which goes with achievement, and with it went my bashfulness.

When they ran a show in which first prize was to go for the best-decorated wheel, I entered my name. Decorating was not in my line, but I tried because I felt lucky. I persuaded Monte Scott to loan me his wheel, the finest in the country, and trimmed it with roses from the yards of our neighbors. I was a proud young man but an awful show-off. We paraded the streets of Providence at night with torchlights, and I passed the judges' stand confident of success, but Will Bitzer was not called. Thoroughly abashed, I went home, deflated and overcome with mortification. The next morning the first person I saw at the shop was another cousin, Dick Strobel, perusing the morning paper as though the world hadn't stood still last night.

"Whoopie!" he cried out. "It says here Will Bitzer wins

first prize!" After that, I considered myself a big shot and did
a lot of bragging. Naturally I antagonized many who might
otherwise have been my friends, so they set out to teach me
a lesson. The next race I pedaled, I found I was getting nowhere. I suspected there was something wrong with the
wheel. Something suddenly snapped and I felt myself flying into space over the handlebars, and the next instant I lost
consciousness. I suffered a nasty scar under the chin: the handlebars had cut through to the bone and I still have the scar to
remind me of my youthful experience. Then I found out the
truth: a string had been added to the base of the back wheel
in such a manner that it would work its way around and the
wheel grow taut. Some competitors had done it to deflate my
ego, but they hadn't considered I might get hurt. So I decided
against tempting fate with further bicycle races. Anyway we
were moving. John Bitzer had been transferred to the Gorham
Company's shop in New York, and our new home was a flat
on 114th Street, uptown, a block away from beautiful Morn-
ingside Park.

In 1894, after Father died, I decided to give up the trade of
silversmith and make a life of my own. I went first to Cooper
Union and then to the Magic Introduction Company. Now I
was a moving-picture cameraman, who had just filmed his first
war.

By the time I got out of the hospital, Nora had found a flat
on West Twelfth Street—four rooms facing the street, a bath-
tub in the kitchen and a toilet in the hall. We furnished it together, which was excellent therapy for me. It was the first
home I could call my own, and it was very comfortable. Two
heads on one pillow meant the joy of a new life together. If

Nora's faults were worrisome, her virtues were many. She kept the flat spotless, and my clothes clean and in repair. My chief worry was her drinking. There was always plenty of beer around; she bought it by the two-quart can, called a "growler." If I came home and found she had taken too much drink, she would deny it saying, "I work hard and I was a wee bit overheated."

"Did you save some for me, Muffin?"

The question of marriage never came up. When she suspected me of cheating or drinking too much, she became a tigress, little as she was. Everyone sympathized with my plight, but secretly I rejoiced that someone cared enough to slip the yoke over my neck. We agreed that I should turn my paycheck over to her each week, keeping any overtime for myself. She banked any money she herself earned, paid the bills from my salary, and banked the surplus in our joint account. I could have money anytime I needed it, but she handled the purse strings. I cared so little for money, it even bored me to handle it, and as my overtime money sufficed for my daily needs, I enjoyed hearing her rattle on about how much she saved.

FIVE

Biograph Moves to Fourteenth Street

1903

When I was able to go back to work, they put me on the off-color pictures, the Mutoscopes, because they were made quickly and there was no "location" work. We now made them at night, and we used Cooper-Hewitt mercury vapor lamps for studio illumination. Fred Wake and myself made the Mutoscopes for the arcade machines, not to be shown on the screen. Some of the most popular of these used the Turkish-harem theme. For this we used tall men and Fred Balshofer was often our high mogul, despoiler of pure womanhood. Two potted palms, a mattress covered with dozens of pillows, some drapes, and a couple of scimitars. In stalks the sultan to claim the girl for his lustful purpose, and the camera grinds on . . .

I was always ready, however, to go on the road when an important "News Happening" with visual appeal took place. On September 8, 1900, a hurricane broke out along the Texas coast, including the counties of Galveston and Brazoria. For destructiveness it was without precedent on the North American continent. At two o'clock on Saturday morning the wind started to rise. It lashed the waves of the Gulf of Mexico into tremendous fury, causing them to rise to all but mountainous heights. With combined force from the wind traveling at eighty-four miles an hour, the water poured in. For four hours the city of Galveston was one black hell, and those near the beaches raced to the highest spots of the city for refuge. Up and up the waves crawled; all connections with the mainland —telephone, telegraph, railroad tracks, and bridges—were torn away, while forty thousand people cowered in terror for eight long hours of darkness. Hundreds at a time, dwellings went down like houses built of cards. As soon as news of the storm was flashed across the country, relief agencies began to mobilize. Voluntary contributions came in by the thousands; food, medicine, and clothing were piled into trains on their way to bring aid to the survivors.

The Hearst newspapers were the first to get started. They telephoned Mr. McCutcheon at Biograph, asking if he had a man who could cover the story from the motion-picture angle, and I was assigned. The train was to leave from Hoboken within a few hours and I had no time to lose. All I took with me was a suitcase containing raincoat and boots, which I always had ready for any exigency, and the new light portable Biograph camera and its tripod. In Hoboken they told me the train had already taken off, but I ran out into the yards to check and found the train delayed in getting started because of faulty brakes. As I was the only motion-picture cameraman to cover the story, I needed every bit of luck I could get. The New York *Journal* Special Relief Train, consisting of two Pullman sleepers and an express car, left the Delaware Lackawanna and Western depot at 7 p.m. on September 12, 1900.

In the sleeping car were twenty-eight doctors and nurses, fully equipped for the emergency assignment. In the express car were boxes of medicine and barrels of food for the injured —everything you could think of, from champagne to adhesive plasters. The volunteers had been instructed to meet at the *Journal* office as early as 5 p.m. I was now using the light de luxe Biograph camera, which made it possible for me to cover disaster territory better, but this still allowed me little time to mobilize; anyway I made it.

We traveled over the Wabash road from Buffalo to St. Louis, then over the Iron Mountain system from St. Louis to Houston, arriving on September 13. Here we got our first glimpse of the storm center at Texas City, which was as close as our train could take us. All bridges had been washed away and tracks demolished. I was inured to the acid smells of the train and the sickening odor of lunch baskets with spoiled food. During the trip I scarcely ate, as I felt every bite of food should be saved for starving survivors. Not so the volunteers, who helped themselves to the best and slept much of the time. I watched the doctors opening their medicine bags and examining the instruments in anticipation of the task before them. I formed a great dislike for the cold-blooded way in which they did everything. It never occurred to me that, when I puttered with my camera, I too was performing in like manner. At Texas City a few of us donned boots and raincoats and jumped into the first rowboat that would take us over. The volunteers crossed later on the regular ferry.

It was evening when we made the trip across. The water was thick with the stinking remains of dogs, chickens, cows, horses, and the bodies of human beings. The shores, as far as the eye could see, looked like massive piles of timber, scattered and torn. A cloud of smoke, indicating a fire, could be seen not far off. On landing we ran along the beach and came on piles of sand in every direction; bodies washed up by the tide had been buried. We could see the stark, swollen bodies of women and children lined up, awaiting burial. Farther out, more bodies could be seen which would soon float in.

The stench was overpowering. We headed for the fire, and when we saw men feeding the flames with timber from the wrecked homes, we realized it was a funeral pyre. In this combustible heap, volunteer firemen were burning one thousand bodies. It had been difficult to find men who would bury the bloated bodies, so the city had ordered that the dead be loaded upon barges, weighted, and cast into the sea. Evidently the bodies had not been properly weighted, for they floated back to the shore in hundreds. Then it was decided the only way to guarantee permanent disposal was a vast funeral pyre. Oil was poured and then set ablaze by men with torches. We shot pictures of this, but doubted if the public would be receptive to viewing it. This blaze was so terrific that it gave strong light and deep shadows, and seemed as unreal as Dante's Inferno.

There was nothing more we could do until morning, so we went to the Tremont Hotel, which had been spared. The volunteers arrived soon after us, and the Hall High School was turned over to them for a hospital. Here twenty-eight volunteer medical faces fell, for they found they could do nothing for the dead. As for the living, their troubles were mental, not physical. The great tragedy had exacted deep losses of family. While individuals eagerly narrated the loss of cows, horses, or household pets, they remained silent when asked about a wife or child they had lost. There were no tears: they were beyond tears, still in a state of shock.

In the face of this tragedy, we now heard rumors of thieves and ghouls roaming about the city, robbing the dead of valuables. Fingers had been cut off for rings and ears for earrings. Even an arm had been cut off a dead girl to get the diamond bracelet she was wearing. These vultures worked fast. Captain Rafferty, in charge, ordered all his men to shoot at sight all persons found despoiling the dead. One hundred and twenty-five ghouls were exterminated before the island was cleared of them. I listened to the group in the hotel lobby until late at night, then turned in for rest.

Next morning I was up early and on the job. It was difficult to move or breathe with death on all sides. No one seemed entirely sane. There was madness in the air. The wonder was that a single soul was left to give evidence of the sudden disaster. Along the waterfront, human bodies were floating around like corkwood. When the waves washed up bodies, they seemed alive, as their arms seemed to stretch out for help. This affected me severely when some tiny child, so doll-like, would come into view and spread out its arms. The burying parties were too busy for sentiment, and after a while they became so conditioned to their work that they even laughed and joked as they went about the gruesome tasks. They bandaged their mouths and noses with cotton cloth saturated with disinfectants. They had to be relieved every hour by other volunteers as the sun's heat took its toll.

General McKidden had issued an order prohibiting the use of cameras, and the troops were instructed to shoot looters. I went to headquarters and explained that motion pictures would help to get aid for these stricken people. I finally got permission and I was able to continue. I pinned one permit on my back and one on my chest, where all could see, for I was taking no chances with these soldiers. They were within their rights to shoot marauders, and these were desperate days.

Relief came pouring in from all directions. Clara Barton,

who for fifty years had been upon every great disaster scene, ministering to the suffering, arrived with her Red Cross. President McKinley had dispatched vessels with government supplies. Finally there were more doctors and nurses than patients.

In 1903 Biograph moved to a more spacious building, an old private brownstone house, which was to be our new home at 11 East Fourteenth Street. We made that address famous in motion-picture history.

Henry Norton Marvin was still vice president of the American Biograph and Wallace McCutcheon, Sr., was the director of our pictures. Then McCutcheon developed a sickness which kept him to his bed. A temporary director had to be found quickly—no simple matter. Several men were hired in succession, but their stays were brief. The first man was very methodical. I do not recollect his name, but he was impossible. In the morning he would enter abruptly and go straight to his desk, where he would immediately take care of any letters and directives for the day. On leaving his office to start the day's work in the ballroom studio, where we would be shooting, he would consult his watch and then make out a card telling the exact time he would return. Then he would pompously proceed to impress us with his efficiency by giving orders.

"What is all this string doing here?" he demanded. "Pick it up and tie it together, and then put it away some place where you will have it when you need it." Or "What are all these nails doing scattered about? Pick them up and straighten the bent ones and put them where you will be able to find a nail when you need one!" Very, very efficient. And his pictures were as prim and stupid as you'd expect from such a character.

Funny though, most of the staff were impressed with this

and thought he gave the place class, but somehow I didn't feel right about it. My word carried weight in those days, so I sent a wire to Wally McCutcheon, Jr., who was out West, asking him to come home and fill his father's boots until the time when he would be well enough to stand on his own.

Wally came at once. He was a gay young blade whose brilliance showed best when surrounded by a bevy of girls. Unfortunately, in his eagerness to please the ladies, he forgot all about the business of the day. We got very little work done, so he was next to get sacked.

Our pictures were now becoming so poor that we grasped at any straw to find a man to direct for us. Then Stanner E. V. Taylor came along. He had written several scenarios and stories, and was an Englishman with lofty manners. He was always making speeches of what he could and would do. We were awed to some extent, but not quite convinced.

Marion Leonard was then the best actress on the screen. From the time of Taylor's entrance into our company, she became a changed woman. He courted her with tales of his rise in the world through his writings and ability as a director. Marion faltered, and then she married him. Taylor's swan song was *Over the Hills to the Poorhouse*, which nearly sent us all there.

The already impoverished company now gave up the struggle to the Empire Trust Company, which controlled it. George Blanchard, who had been put in by Henry Marvin, was removed as president and in his stead George E. Van Guysling was appointed. He turned out to be another efficiency man, more careful of the behavior of others than of his own. This made J. J. Kennedy, the president of Empire Trust, our temporary head, because, after six months' trial, Van

Guysling was removed. R. H. Hammer was made permanent president, and he remained in that capacity until 1913, when I left Biograph with Mr. Griffith. Arthur Marvin, brother of Henry Marvin, was kept on, for he was a good cameraman, something no studio could do without.

The storerooms at 11 East Fourteenth Street were packed to overflowing with props, furniture, and scenery we had used in our little playlets. The lumber and other material were fire hazards, and we were warned by the fire department to get rid of them. The trouble was how to get them hauled away. In taking inventory, we found we had stored leftover kegs of gunpowder. How was I going to get rid of it? I could not throw it in the furnace and blow up the place, and dared not throw it in the ash can, so it remained where it was until we could get rid of it ourselves.

There were now many little film companies springing up, known as independents, while Biograph, under Mr. Kennedy, had now joined with Edison and others in the Motion Picture Patents Company, also known as "The Trust." The little independent companies would quickly copy anything we did that the public seemed to favor. If we made a battle picture, they would make one too. One company had even dug up the same trenches we had used for a scene in Fort Lee. We had filled them in for the landowner when we had finished, only to see an independent dig them up again a few days later.

Adam Kessel, one of the independents, was a great friend of mine. We trusted and respected each other, and he would often drop in on me and talk shop. His company had forgotten to order gunpowder, and one weekend, with a Monday holiday also intervening, he was at a loss how to get the picture started. He came to me at night and implored me to help him.

"Can you get me some gunpowder, Billy?" he begged. We were all struggling to survive, and at least on the working level we tried to help each other. Having the keys to our storage room, I pretended to see what I could let him have, though I wanted him to take all of it. I knew the company would object to giving anything to an adversary, but on the other hand we would be in trouble over this dangerous stuff at the next building inspection. His men came to take away the gunpowder, and I was rid of a big responsibility. Kessel took out his checkbook and asked me to name the price.

"Your money is no good, Addie," I assured him. "Put your checkbook away."

"You may be sorry, Billy, when your boss discovers this, so I will give you a signed check and you can fill in the amount later. You saved us two days' delay, and we might have lost the release of the picture."

I didn't want the check, but felt guilty for helping a rival company. I put the check in my pocket as a souvenir, a reminder I could jokingly pull his leg about. Much later I wanted his laboratory man, Abe Sholtz, and Kessel refused, for Abe was the most skilled lab man in the business. Then I thought of the old check, so I dug it out and wrote in the name Abe Sholtz where the amount of money should have been.

"Billy, what on earth is this?" he asked.

"The gunpowder, Addie, remember? It's your turn to do me a favor." And that's how Abe Sholtz came to work in the Biograph laboratory.

There was a lot of speculation among cameramen about the Méliès camera, built in France before 1904. All we could do was guess how he worked out all his film fantasies himself. His magic tricks intrigued cameramen like me who were not permitted to waste company film experimenting. At the end of a film roll, there is always some left over, and this I used for experimental purposes, though I never discovered the secrets of some of the Méliès magic.

It has been asked many times whether Griffith or Bitzer should be credited with the fade-out. It probably should be neither one. This was brought home to me forcibly in the 1930's after I had read Iris Barry's amazingly accurate program notes on Griffith. It seemed strange to me, until I thought about it and came to this conclusion: I had been so preoccupied with the mechanics of the camera that I did not pay much attention to what was later lauded as a marvelous achievement. To me it was just another day's work. If Mr. Griffith asked for some effect, whether a fade-out or whatever, I tried one way or another to produce what he wanted. When it worked successfully, we were hailed as inventors.

No doubt about it, we had seen the fade-out in the early Méliès pictures and forgotten about it. I wasn't especially intrigued when I first saw the Méliès dissolve. I felt that the tremendous possibilities of the movie camera had been barely scratched. After being hailed as the originator of various photographic effects, I had the wind taken out of my sails completely when I found there had been others "originating" the same things. Now I wish to make amends and say we did not create the fade-out. I believe it really was Méliès. God knows the man got little enough for his efforts, including his famous *A Trip to the Moon* in 1902, and he died in want.

Billy Bitzer in 1898 with the bulky Biograph camera (a detail from
the endpapers)

The four founders of the American Mutoscope & Biograph Company in 1895. From the left, Henry N. Marvin, William Kennedy Laurie Dickson, Herman Casler, and Elias B. Koopman (who first employed Bitzer). Their initials make up the K.M.C.D. syndicate

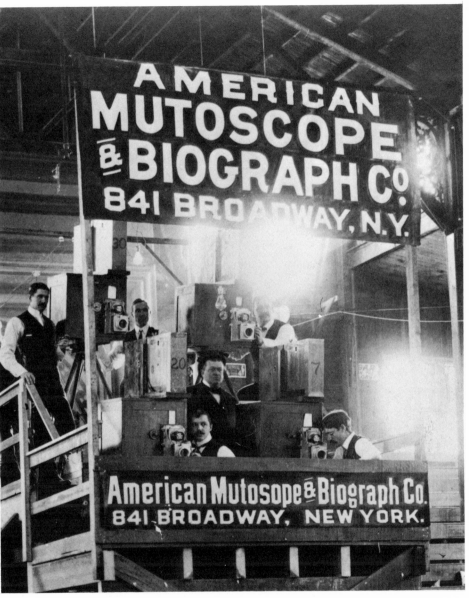

Four Biograph cameras set up to film the Jeffries-Sharkey fight in 1899, at the Coney Island Athletic Club. Bitzer is beside the camera at lower left; Henry Marvin is the tall man in shirt sleeves, standing with a stop watch. The heavy-set man standing in center may be William A. Brady, the showman who hired Biograph to film the fight

Rare photo of the unfinished outdoor Biograph studio atop 841 Broadway. The hatless man with folded arms is W. K. L. Dickson, with Arthur Marvin, Henry's brother, on the right. The camerahouse and stage are set on rails, to be moved with the sun

The same studio in March 1897, showing a movie being made. This photo appeared in *Scientific American*, from which it is reproduced

Early porno, *Birth of the Pearl*, a Mutoscope shocker (see Bitzer's comment, page 10)

SOLE OWNERS.
THE BIOGRAPH.—THE MUTOSCOPE.

FOREIGN CONNECTIONS.
LONDON.—PARIS.
AMSTERDAM.
BERLIN.—VIENNA.
JOHANNESBURG.
BRUSSELS—BOMBAY.

GEO. R. BLANCHARD, President.
WM. H. KIMBALL, 1st Vice "
H. N. MARVIN., 2nd Vice "
E. B. KOOPMAN, London Director

TECHNICIANS:
HERMAN CASLER.
WM. K·L. DICKSON.

TELEPHONE: 1860-18th ST.
CABLE ADDRESS: "MUTO."
LIEBER CODE

American Mutoscope and Biograph Company,

841 Broadway,

New York, September 25, *1900*

To Managers of Theatres:—

You will note by the attached clipping that one

of our operators has just returned from Galveston. He was one of the

first on the ground and worked with a special Government permit.

We have developed his first installment of films and find

them not only excellent photographically but VERY SENSATIONAL— rescue

parties bringing out bodies, burying the dead, etc.

A quick booking of the American Biograph will give you a

great opportunity for press work.

Yours very truly,
Wallace M. Cutcheon

Mgr. Biograph Department.

Wallace McCutcheon's letter to managers about Bitzer's films of the
Galveston disaster (see pages 45–50)

Bitzer using the lighter, more portable Biograph camera in 1905 to film U.S. Army field artillery maneuvers

$\mathcal{D}.\ \mathcal{W}.\ \mathcal{G}riffith$
1 9 0 8

At the time of our Biograph discontent, a young actor was making his way into pictures. The first professional name he used was Lawrence Carter, and later it became Lawrence or Larry Griffith. My attention was directed to him because one day I was called on the carpet for having allowed him to be photographed in such a manner that he seemed to have three or four arms instead of the usual two. The fault was not mine, but his. He acted with so many gestures because, I later learned, that had been his stage style in costume dramas with Nance O'Neill and other stars of the theater. The second time I encountered him, he overacted the part of a bartender, so in order to save myself trouble, I asked him if he was trying to get me fired, or wasn't he aware his mugging was taking the action away from the lead? He confided that a friend had told him that was the way to act in pictures, but now that I had brought it to his attention, he wouldn't do it again. He told me he was a writer, accepting movie jobs for the money. He asked my advice about directing work. I advised him against it, for I couldn't see how a man who wasn't a passable actor could direct a flock of geese. I also told him if he tried for director and didn't make good, his acting career in our studio would be over. I had already seen enough ambitious people turn out pictures that failed.

Lee Dougherty, the Biograph scenario writer, is the man to whom Griffith really owed the chance to become a director. It was he who interceded with the powers-that-be and had faith in Griffith's talent, which I was unable to see. When the offer to direct came in the spring of 1908, Griffith had the good sense to think of what I had told him. He asked to be kept on as an actor if he failed in the new job, and they gave him their promise.

Then they put him to work first on the off-color pictures, the Mutoscopes. Linda Arvidson was also working in these pictures, flaunting a wicked petticoat in her Swedish way. She had arrived at the studio concurrently with Griffith and was secretly his wife, but none of us suspected it. It was after the dismissal of Stanner E. V. Taylor that Griffith was given his first real chance. The picture was *The Adventures of Dollie*. Arthur Marvin was assigned to the camerawork on this, which was photographed in the daytime. I remained with Fred Wake, shooting the off-color Mutoscopes at night.

Griffith was always a great hand at asking questions. He came to ask me where there was a river just large enough to carry a child downstream in a barrel. I suggested the Bronx River. Not entirely satisfied, he consulted others; first the Hackensack River was suggested and then Marvin advised him to use Sound Beach, Connecticut.

One evening as Nora and I had just finished supper, I heard

a call from below. I looked over the second-floor banister and saw it was Griffith.

"So there you are," he called, as he mounted the stairs. "I've been looking for you. No one seemed to know your address. Hope you don't mind my barging in on you like this, but I need your help."

"What's the use telling you anything?" I replied in an injured tone. "You'll end up by taking someone else's advice anyway."

"But as you see, I've come for your help," he said.

Then I showed him to our room, where I gave him the advice he wanted. First we went over the story together. It ran: "On the lawn of a country residence we find Father, Mother, and little Dollie. In front of the grounds there flows a picturesque stream to which Mother and Dollie go to watch the boys fishing . . . A gypsy approaches them, offering his baskets for sale. They refuse to buy, which raises his ire, and he seizes the woman's purse and is off, but the husband hears her cries and rushes to her aid, and with a heavy lash whips the gypsy, who leaves, vowing revenge. The family returns to the lawn, where Father plays battledore and shuttlecock with Dollie, and Mother returns to the house. Mother calls Father into the house, leaving Dollie alone, and the gypsy runs off with the child, hiding her in a water cask in his camp. Placing the cask in the back of their wagon, the gypsies speed away, but as they ford the stream, the cask falls off into the water and is carried away—first over the waterfalls, then through the rapids, and on, until finally it enters the quiet cove of the first scene, where the boys are fishing. The boys break open the cask and rescue little Dollie; they call for Mother and Father, and there is a happy reunion."

On the back of a laundry cardboard, I wrote down some of the elements of this story:

HEART INTEREST	DRAMA	DANGER	COMEDY	RESCUE
Love	Gypsy menace	Suspense	Have cask hit and upset man in boat	Boys hear girl's cry within cask
Happy family		Stealing child		
	Mother and gypsy struggle			
Child and father playing		Shut into cask	Have boys' fish lines snarled up	Break cask open and girl emerges
	Father whips gypsy	Fall from wagon		

Then I cautioned Griffith to be careful when shooting the house in his picture not to make it too small and faraway, as had happened to me in photographing *Over the Hills to the Poorhouse*. Also to look into the camera and see that there were no open spaces left on either side, but to keep all the pictures close at hand. He expressed the wish that I would be his cameraman. I told him I appreciated his confidence in me, but Arthur Marvin was a good boy and, if he ever refused to do as told, get him a bottle of beer which Arthur and I were both fond of and he would be able to get most anything he wanted from him. We parted with a friendly handshake, and somehow I liked that man Griffith.

On location Arthur Marvin and Griffith got on all right, but Arthur was amazed at Griffith's self-confidence. Finally Griffith told him he had got advice from me, which called for two reactions from Arthur: first he bawled me out; then he made Griffith the goat for plenty of beer.

The leading lady was Linda Arvidson, who played the part

of Dollie's mother. Griffith had asked for her, and he was given permission. Miss Arvidson, as we knew her then, was a woman of admirable character. While in California with a stock company in which they both played, they had struck up a friendship which had culminated in their secret marriage. Theirs was a romance which had its birth in Griffith's interest in poems, of which Miss Arvidson had a fund of knowledge. We none of us suspected they knew each other outside of studio walls, for they were never seen either entering or leaving the studio together.

The Adventures of Dollie was good, but at first the exhibitors did not like it. Biograph decided to release the picture anyway, in order to get some of their money back. The public took an entirely different view of it. They liked it and told their friends to be sure and see it. Then, of course, the exhibitors demanded more pictures of a like nature. Griffith had fulfilled his promise. Biograph signed him to his first contract as director in August 1908.

Just before that, we worked on our first film together, *A Calamitous Elopement*, which Biograph released in August. All I remember about it is that we shot some action on the street in front of 11 East Fourteenth. I also recall that Griffith acted the part of a policeman in his own film and that Linda Arvidson played the eloping heroine. With this picture, the team of Griffith–Bitzer came into existence. In all the years we worked together, even after I finally left Biograph with Mr. Griffith, there was never a written contract, only a handshake and our trust in each other.*

From the time Griffith started directing motion pictures, he

* Apparently Mr. Bitzer forgot about his three-year contract from 1913 to 1916, a copy of which is in MOMA Archives.

worked continually and incessantly. He never took vacations, though he had the right to. A vacation would have annoyed him; he liked his work too well. After he got into his stride, we occasionally made as high as five one-reelers in five days— one a day from Monday through Friday! He was persistent and never loafed on the job. Compared to previous directors, he was a pretty hard man to work for, but we accepted it because he worked even harder than we did.

He often spent evenings looking at movies. On Saturday afternoons, he sometimes asked me to go to the nickelodeon with him to test the audience reaction to our pictures. At the nickelodeons on the Lower East Side of New York, we noticed that immigrants learned English by reading the titles aloud.

Under his direction there seemed to be much more work on location. We had to develop a large crew who built outdoor stage sets on wooden platforms. Nora often came along to the village of Cuddebackville, New York, which she loved. As this was the first location we went on after Griffith became my director, it stands out prominently in my mind. The stories we were doing had to have a mountainous locale. This was the ideal spot for it, as the sloping hills looked like mountains when photographed against the sunset.

We always stopped at the Cuddeback Inn, run by my friend Mr. Predmore, where we would gather at night for rest and recreation. Evening found the men actors downstairs for a game of craps which lasted well into the night. I was too tired after a hard day lugging the camera to give much thought to anything but rest.

Once the game lasted so late and got so noisy that I donned my trousers to investigate and complain. I soon cooled off, for there upon his knees was Griffith, playing the game in a most skilled manner. He would watch a man win three or four times, then bet all he had against his winning the next pot. The law of percentages was with him and he came out ahead. I went quietly back to my room, wondering where he had picked up his skill.

The eastern sky is a sharp color in the morning, a new color in the afternoon, and each season has different light. Fort Lee, New Jersey, was an ideal place for movies, for it encompassed everything we needed, such as overnight lodging and proximity to the New York studio, and most of all, hearty breakfasts at Murphy's. We got the best photographic results in early morning, without shadows. It is then the light sharpens the distant hills and accentuates the blackness of objects in the foreground.

Before Griffith began directing, he had sold some stories to Biograph. In a short time his attempt at directing revealed some of his revolutionary ideas, not perhaps as many as he would have wished, for he had to buck the you-can't-do-that brigade. Before his arrival I, as cameraman, was responsible for everything except the immediate hiring and handling of the actor. Soon it was his say whether the lights were bright enough, or if the make-up was right. If the face was powdered up with pink powder, the eyelashes black and beaded with melted mascara, and the lips painted red, it was all right with me. I never bothered how they looked, just so I could see their faces in my aperture. A cameraman had enough to do watching rapidity of action and keeping the hand-cranked camera going at a steady pace to prevent the film from buckling.

We used the slow emulsion orthochromatic negative Eastman film, which was all right in bright sunlight, as it gave bright color values and cloud effects when used with an orange ray filter. It was 1 ½ times as fast as ordinary Kodak film, but it was not so good later in the day, with the low-key light Mr. Griffith preferred. The front office complained: film was too expensive to waste on foolishness. To them the bright sunlight was the only tried-and-true method, and if I wanted to keep my job, I had better listen to the office and not to Griffith.

When he moved his camera closer to the players, it was definitely vetoed by the front office. In order to view the little postage-stamp, upside-down image through the little brass tube, a cameraman had to virtually stand on his head. You see, there was no lens calibration on the camera. My lens was mounted upon a plain flange which made it easier to focus when we worked a little away from the subject. In moving closer we always took a chance of being out of focus. It wasn't all beer and skittles, and it wasn't without sweat. I was dressed down many times by Biograph for using Griffith innovations, but the pictures were better under the new technique and Biograph sales were up by leaps and bounds. Finally even the front office stopped griping.

Griffith generally got what he wanted, one way or another, but it was mainly through his infectious enthusiasm. Sailing along at an even keel, rarely ever perturbed, certainly not temperamental, so that when a blow-up did come, whether it was just a bawling out of the players or taking to task a single actor to the extent of having it out with fisticuffs, it was not soon forgotten. Griffith handled himself real well. Little wonder, for he shadowboxed a lot when I first knew him, and later there was usually some ex-pug around among the extras—a Spike Robinson and even Kid McCoy—that he privately boxed with to keep in shape. His muscles were well developed in his early formative years and he never let them get flabby. There never was a question as to his leadership, and that is why he was always "Mister Griffith" to all of us. Once he assumed the job of director, none of us ever called him David or Dave, though his wife and his old friends still called him Larry. I mention this as it is one of the frequent questions I am asked.

In November 1908 Griffith began a series of domestic comedies similar to Pathé Frères' French comedies with Max Linder. They were called the Jones family series; Florence Lawrence, John Compson, Mary Pickford, and Billy Quirk were the principal players. Up to June 1909, there were no theater (non-Mutoscope) pictures taken at Biograph by other than D. W. Griffith. After June 1909, Frank Powell began as the second director, with Arthur Marvin on camera. Every Biograph picture carried our marker—the large *AB* placed on each set to ensure identification of our property. It was a shield against duplication or theft.

If you look at the list of popular actors of the old days, you will note they were mostly big apes of men. There were Alan Hal, Lionel Barrymore, Lell Henderson, William J. Butler, Charles West, Jack Mulhall, and our own big handsome Arthur Johnson. Then there was muscle man Mack Sennett, who came to Biograph looking for any kind of job: handling props, packing film, or acting. He was just the sort of man we needed around to play cops or a mug. But a dress suit looked like a suit of armor on him, for he was made like a box. His head seemed to sit on his square shoulders without a neck, there was no visible waistline, and seen from any angle, he was square from his head to his bulldog shoes.

Owen Moore and Arthur Johnson were handsome men who

looked great in costumes or dress suits. In one film Marion Leonard was the bride and Owen Moore the groom. There was a domestic scene where his mother-in-law, played by Kate Bruce, nags at him, and then his bride complains he doesn't hang up his clothes, so he gets angry and returns to his pals at the Union League Club. The return scene was to be the highlight of the picture. When Owen enters the room, every man rises from his sitting position and raises his glass, welcoming Owen back into the fold. Owen looked terrific in any clothes he wore, as did Arthur Johnson, who played his pal. But the rest of the actors, especially Mack Sennett, looked like they came out of Kane's warehouse.

Griffith was greatly dissatisfied with the awkwardness of the scene, and said he would leave the set while the actors worked it out. He made them an offer—if the scene worked, every actor's pay would be raised from five dollars to ten for the day. I think it was Arthur Johnson who found the solution. When Griffith returned, they hoisted Owen Moore on their shoulders, carried him around the room, stood him on top of the table, raised their glasses, and yelled:

> *Biograph, Biograph,*
> *Hah! Hah! Hah!*
> *Ten dollars, ten dollars,*
> *Rah! Rah! Rah!*

Griffith said it achieved exactly the effect he wanted. So they repeated it with even more enthusiasm for my camera.

Henry B. Walthall, who later achieved stardom as the "Little Colonel" in *The Birth of a Nation*, was loved by everyone and was a fine actor. His performances were well ahead of his time. Wally, as he was affectionately called, had that sort of lazy Southern laxity. It was hard for him to be on time, but he always had ingratiating and convincing alibis for being late. All of us, especially Griffith, looked forward to his entrance for that reason. Both Griffith and Walthall were Southerners, and I believe the latter gave Griffith just that touch of home he needed to relax.

James Kirkwood and Mary Pickford made their debut at Biograph in the same week. According to Biograph records, Mary appeared in *Her First Biscuits* before we made *The Lonely Villa*, in which Mary played the child of Marion Leonard and Kirkwood played a robber. Kirkwood had dropped in on Griffith, an old friend and fellow actor. He had heard somewhere about his being a movie director and thought it would be fun to look him up and rib him. Griffith prevailed upon him to put on whiskers, step into the picture, and go to work. In a spirit of fun the well-known stage actor, James Kirkwood, entered where other, lesser actors had feared to tread. He stayed with us when he found the money was regular and he could live cheaper than on the road with a show.

Mary Pickford was awfully cute with her childlike ways and curls. There was something about the way she would enact the parts given her that was different from any previous actress. It was her sincerity, which you couldn't help liking, and it was also how lovely she looked. She was a marvelous photographic subject and an untiring worker. It has been said that all she had were two dimples, curls, and a lot of luck. Don't you believe it, for there were many other girls who had all that, but they were drab personalities beside Mary. Mary would have succeeded in any career she wished to follow. This business of make-up, for instance—none of us gave it much thought, but Mary first used one make-up and, when she saw herself on screen, would reblend it and come to me.

"Do you think this is better, Billy?" she would ask. Under

the lights we would study it as if we were artists mixing colors for their canvas. "Do you think I should put in a little more yellow? More pink?" Mary had a flexible, imaginative mind. A story idea sent her scurrying for a scrap of paper to make notes, which she would later turn into scenarios and the extra paycheck. Among the early successes I know Mary contributed to were *The Awakening, Caught in the Act, Getting Even, The Girl of Yesterday, The Alien, Granny, Fate's Decree*, and the never-to-be-forgotten *Lena and the Geese*. She also played the lead in many of these.

Mary's mother, Lottie Smith, took charge of her personal effects. Mrs. Smith kept her daughter's fine hair groomed to glossy silk and in rag curlers until time to shoot the action. Offstage Mary dressed in pastel shades mostly. Her salary was small at first, but her mother, a good business manager, soon changed that. Griffith was impressed and pleased.

Mary's first love scene was a fatal day. Griffith sent everyone home but the four persons needed—the two actors, Mary Pickford and Owen Moore; the cameraman; and the director. Mr. Griffith started coaching Mary: "You are no longer a child. You are a woman. See that man over there? You love him dearly. Now walk over to him and throw your arms around him. He has been away from you for a long time and has just returned to you. Kiss him with all the warmth you have in you. And do it as though you meant it."

As he spoke, Mary looked over at the man and he looked at her. She crossed the set in a flash, right into the arms of Owen Moore. The air was charged with a beautiful four-letter word —love. Griffith sensed it at once and called "Cut!" to me. They stood apart, just looking at each other, sort of puzzled at the suddenness of the impact. It wasn't easy for her to accept. Handsome as Owen was, and charming, he had already developed a penchant for liquor, and she knew it. We figured she would be too smart to get deeply involved.

Griffith took advantage of Mary's romance to make her act with more spirit. He'd say, "Mary, why waste time with that wastrel, Owen Moore? If he thought anything at all about you, he wouldn't be drinking at a bar, he'd be right here."

"Don't you dare say anything against Owen!" the spunky Mary defended her choice. As her eyes welled with angry tears, Griffith looked away, grimly satisfied. This was the look he wanted in the scene we were going to film. "Camera!" he called. Without hesitation Mary delivered exactly what he wanted.

It was said that Griffith made puppets of his people. The answer is that, if need be, he would play one against the other to whip them into giving the best they had. He was a man whose job came first, and in his mind we were there for one reason only—making pictures.

Nature created man with an appetite for the opposite sex. It would be false for me to say Griffith had no women in his life. Girls simply adored him and few concealed their infatuation. Girls could have cluttered his life had he allowed them to, but he didn't have the time. The actress he favored wasn't necessarily the star, as the public might suppose, it most likely was a girl who kept in the background. A player named Dorothy West was the first to endanger his marriage. No one suspected an affair except Miss Arvidson, who (we now knew) was his wife. She didn't take kindly to her rival at all. In fact, there was hell to pay and so much fireworks that Dorothy knew if she stayed, her life would not be worth it. So it wasn't too long before Dorothy departed.

SEVEN

Biograph in Hollywood
1910

Perhaps because he was a Southerner, Griffith had a great dislike of cold weather and really hated the New York winters. In the fall of 1909, he began working on Henry Marvin and J. J. Kennedy, telling them he knew every segment of California from personal experience and that he could guarantee Biograph would benefit from the sunny weather and picturesque settings. Finally, in December, while we were still making *The Newlyweds* at the Fourteenth Street studio, word came that we could take off for California in a few days. It seems that Mr. Hammer, the new president, had gone on to the Coast and made the arrangements beforehand.

In January 1910, the Biograph Company set foot in Hollywood for the first time. Our studio was a vacant lot at the corner of Grand Avenue and Washington Street, with a loft nearby to store properties, which were the responsibility of Bobby Harron and Johnny Mahr. On the lot we constructed a large wooden platform and covered this area with white cotton sheets on pulleys, so that we could adjust the amount of sunlight needed for the camera. As I recall, there were no dressing rooms for the players, though I believe we set up temporary tents while there. We all stayed at the Alexandria Hotel, but there were a lot of side trips, too. We went to the San Gabriel Mission to make *The Thread of Destiny*, and to Santa Monica to photograph *The Unchanging Sea*.

There were already several movie companies in California. Selig, whose leading player was Hobart Bosworth, had been the first to arrive in 1907. My good friend Adam Kessel and his partner Charles Bauman had also come out in 1909. As an independent company, they wanted to get away from the patents group and were already set up in Edendale; their location later was taken over by Mack Sennett and the Keystone comedies.

We made dozens of films in California between January and April, after which we returned to New York. The picture I remember best is *Two Brothers*, a Mexican romance. We traveled down to San Juan Capistrano, about sixty miles south of Los Angeles, to use the old mission and its environs as background. The company included Mary Pickford, Owen Moore, Arthur Johnson, Henry Walthall, Kate Bruce, W. Christie Miller, Bobby Harron, and some rodeo cowboys we had just engaged.

Griffith was intrigued by the legend of the swallows, which are said to return to this mission every Saint Joseph's Day (March 19), and also by the ruins of the old mission, built originally in the form of a cross. It was made of adobe mud by Indians and Spanish monks. It had withstood earthquakes and was said to be haunted by a dark-robed Franciscan ghost.

We traveled down in two trains—a special coach and a combined baggage-and-horse car. It was after midnight when we arrived in San Juan Capistrano, in a raw downpour. The rain was something that had escaped our consideration and plans. Arrangements had been made beforehand with the full cooperation of the monks, even to their consenting to the use of church vestments and holy objects in our picture.

Our special train was shunted onto the siding, waiting for the storm to pass. It continued without letup. Owen Moore, growing more and more restive, made a daring attempt to dash out to the inn, carrying his wife, Mary Pickford, in his arms. Soon they were back, laughing and panting, unable to make it. One by one, actors would dart out, girl in arms, amid laughter and delighted shrieks. The men were daring and young, and the girls were willing. There were also our rodeo cowboys, headed by the undaunted champion, Art Accord. Somehow the youngsters all made it to the inn; then the older members were taken up in wagons. Once inside, we found the inn boasted a cheerful fireplace, with logs burning in the grate, low ceilings, and Navajo rugs scattered on the floor.

After two days of continuous downpour, our rooms seemed to wall us in. "Could we accomplish anything now, Billy?" Griffith asked me time after time. A cameraman suddenly becomes the most important man when the weather is bad. The third day found everyone depressed, for it was Easter. Suddenly the rain stopped as abruptly as it had begun.

I stood on the balcony of the Spanish-style inn just before dawn, when suddenly the sun broke through. Then over the brow of the hill some dark figures appeared and seemed headed for the church alongside the old mission. From opposite directions more figures were coming, then a larger group, and between them they were carrying a litter. This was an Indian funeral. It was customary for them to walk all the way from the reservation, carrying their dead. I learned that it was the burial of an old and venerated Indian.

The storm and the rains passed; blue patches appeared in the sky. It was a new day. "Get into your costumes, children," Griffith ordered cheerily. Setting up my camera, I looked around for just the right spot. I was filled with wonder how the huge adobe arches had been constructed. As I looked I could see the receding figures of the Indians returning to their reservation some place over the hills.

Mary Pickford, in Mexican costume, came toward the camera, her hair down the back in rag curlers and a calico sunbonnet tied under her chin. The Mexicans soon spotted Mary; they knew who *she* was. They wanted to watch the fun and see how we made movies. There was outright laughing at our slim vaqueros (cowboys), Henry Walthall and Arthur Johnson, as they mounted their horses.

After some warm-up directions from Griffith, Mary, playing a Mexican bride, had difficulty mounting her burro because the full skirt gave her trouble. Once upon the burro, with her skirts neatly arranged, she took off the sunbonnet, let the rags out of her hair, and then she sat calmly combing it and arranging her curls. Now the natives, who had increased in number, stood off in little groups. No one knew how it started but a murmur arose, swelling louder as angry voices shouted and yelled. Then several Mexican onlookers rushed at W. Christie Miller, who was leading the procession, holding a cross. They flailed their arms threateningly, surrounding the actors who were swinging censers and sprinkling holy water, as directed by Mr. Griffith.

Some natives who had disappeared were soon back, carrying a straw figure on which they had pinned a single accusing sign, JUDAS! They tossed the figure into the doorway of the church, leaving no question as to its meaning. Unwittingly we had committed an unpardonable sin against their faith. We were using the sacred relics with which they had been baptized, married, and would be buried, and despoiled them with our play-acting. Then out of the church came the padre. The jeering intensified. He was a small man with piercing black eyes, a Spaniard, and he demanded respect. He spoke to them in Spanish, and they listened. He said the bishop had agreed to cooperate with us. He told them we meant no harm, but only to spread the word of God by our films and to show people the truth of the Mexican–Indian ceremonies. They seemed to accept this quietly, and then he told them we had with us champion rodeo cowboys, the world's best, and the padre had a proposal. If some of the men would get the little wild bronco that no one had been able to ride, here was a chance to get it broken.

They became very cheerful and animated at this. It took three Mexicans to bring the kicking mustang from the hills. Art Accord came out of the barn, looking like a seedy cowboy with his Stetson hat far back on his head. The Mexicans laughed and obviously expected some fun. With one flying leap, Art was up on the startled critter's back. Man and bronco went down in the soft mud, but soon were up again. It looked bad for our cowboy, but presently Art, with his skill, had the wild one running like a horse should. The people cheered and applauded. When the Accord cowboys saw this, they mounted their horses and put on a rodeo show the watchers would never forget. After that the locals showed us every courtesy and by the time we left Capistrano two days later, our finished picture, *Two Brothers*, was neatly packed in cans.

Other places used for location that first time in California were Sierra Madre for *The Gold Seekers* and *The Twisted Trail;* Pasadena for *Gold Is Not All;* Edendale, where the studio of my friend Adam Kessel was located; and an oil field. One of the longest pictures we made was *Ramona*, with Mary Pickford, filmed in Ventura County. The shortest was *Faithful*, which we shot in Hollywood. I was surprised when Mr. Griffith picked Mack Sennett for this last story, about a half-wit who is rescued by Arthur Johnson from an accident and in gratitude never leaves Johnson out of his sight for a minute. Sennett had always done clowns and cops and mugs, and here he was in a tearjerker. We all thought he acted the part better than anything he had ever done.

Bobby Harron was very excited to be with us on this trip. It was the first time he was away from home, and I felt sort of responsible for him. He had joined Biograph as a boy of ten or eleven in 1907, to do errands and be useful around the place. I had photographed *Bobby's Kodak* (this was before Mr. Griffith arrived on the scene), in which Bobby had his first real part as a child actor. He was one of a large family living in Greenwich Village, helping his father and mother take care of nine brothers and sisters. I remember the day Father William Humphrey of St. Joseph's Church brought him to the Fourteenth Street studio.

"It's about one of the boys in my parish, Bobby Harron," he said. "His father delivers milk and has a hard time making ends meet. Bobby is a good boy, very bright, and he will carry out any task you assign him." So it was settled, and Bobby came to work for us. Every week he turned over his ten-dollar property boy's salary to his family. Whenever Bobby was used in a movie, he made five dollars more a day. Later Bobby brought along a friend of his, Jimmy Smith, who was attending St. Joseph's Academy in Washington Square, conducted by the Christian Brothers. Jimmy developed into one of the best film cutters in the business.

Griffith took an interest in the two youngsters. He remembered when he, too, had been a struggling youth—so had I—and under our guidance Bobby Harron became an outstanding actor. Though he was younger than average for leads, the public took him to their hearts. Jimmy Smith didn't care for acting and called it "sissy stuff." But he learned to put a film together.

In those days, lots of people acted in films who had other jobs around the studio. Don't laugh, but I was too nervous and full of stage fright before a camera. I never would take a chance on acting. My reasons were different from Jimmy's though—I was too self-conscious. I felt at ease behind the camera but not in front of it. By the same token, I never adopted the affected style later used by cameramen, like wearing the cap backward or leather leggings. I felt comfortable wearing a hat, preferably straw. I usually took my coat off, but wore a vest which I found useful for carrying clips, scissors, or other helpful gadgets.

EIGHT

Farewell to Biograph

1913

I will say that the motion-picture world did me a lot of good (unknowingly). I have heard many things about my work which are flattering, but which I was unaware of until I read them in print. When they said of my early photography, "Bitzer was an artist, he followed no accepted school of lighting, neither the German nor French, yet his effects were remarkable," or something along that line, I hied myself to the Metropolitan Museum and asked one of the doormen to direct me to the French school. He finally understood me, even if I didn't know much about art. Of course I did know that the paintings with faces coming out of deep shadows were Rembrandts. I also recognized in the museum a picture that hung in our parlor in my childhood days, "The Angelus," which I thought was painted by Millet and never did learn until later that it was Millay. Perhaps all this is irrelevent, but in my Biograph days I did, however, study closely the lights and shadows of reverse-light pictures, like "The Gleaners," with the foreshadows on the field of stubble. Even with the slow orthochromatic film, which did not permit taking faces with the light behind them (as they would come out pretty black), we succeeded at Biograph, with the aid of a huge bedsheet as a light reflector, in lightening up the faces on the screen in a reverse-sunlight effect. And we even heard exclamations from the front office, "Ah, just like a Millay painting!" Their reaction was all that seemed to matter to us in those days. Let me tell you how I actually discovered this effect.

Owen Moore and Mary Pickford were seated on a bench having their lunch. I was similarly employed, close to my camera. We were over in Fort Lee on location and it was noon. Looking over at the lovers, I noticed the beautiful illumination on their faces and finally figured out that it came from the reflection of the white gravel beneath their feet. I became aware of the total absence of ugly shadows that usually made hollow masks of faces on the screen. Out of curiosity I aimed my camera at them and looked into the ground glass. It sent back a misty rainbow effect, with a haze around the figures. This was caused by the sun shining into the lens. I shaded the lens with my hat and shot a few feet of film experimentally. Mary and Owen were so engrossed in their conversation they had not noticed me. Then came the call, "Back to places, everyone."

I was pleased with the test I had taken, and when I showed it to Mr. Griffith, he was delighted. The reverse-lighting effect was new and splendid. We made several scenes later and again shot into the sun, with my hat to shade the lens. In all we made three scenes without notifying the front office. The first two were great and our hopes soared, but the third was a catastrophe. We had to take the cast back to Fort Lee for another day's retakes and were advised once more to cut out the monkey business. Encouraged by Mr. Griffith, I went ahead with the experiments anyway.

To avoid another accident, I first attached a LePage glue can, which happened to be handy in my workroom, over the small lens of the camera. By cutting out the bottom, it seemed to shade the lens from all sides, solidly, and would not have a tendency to move as my hat apparently had done the third time. I adjusted the glue-can mask, using an incandescent bulb with the lens wide open, of course, to see what I was doing. Next day the conditions were different out in the sunlight. Stopping the lens down had caused the corners of the glue can to darken the corners of the square film.

The laboratory developer phoned me on location next day, suggesting I examine my camera. Something had got mixed up in the aperture plate, as all four edges of the print were fuzzy cutoffs. I talked the situation over with Mr. Griffith and he wasn't too upset.

"Wait until we get back to the studio," he said. "First things come first. Forget it for now."

By the time we returned to Fourteenth Street, the bosses had seen it and we were credited with an innovation. Their pleasure knew no bounds, but it became company merit, company achievement, and company property. They thought the shaded corners took away the hard sharp edges and added class to the picture. I found with repeated tests that I had to use various sized openings to work with the different lens stops, so by getting a larger can and adding an old iris diaphragm from an old eight-by-ten camera, I could control this corner shading. The present-day iris-in and iris-out originated here.

It was apparent to me that Mr. Griffith was more than just another director. To portray joy and sorrow, Griffith studied each new face to find the special character all its own. If talent was recognized, it was because of his discerning knowledge and intuitive perception. No other company had as many actors who developed into stars under his direction: Mary Pickford, Lillian Gish, Blanche Sweet, Dorothy Gish, Mabel Normand, Mae Marsh, Clair MacDowell, Miriam Cooper, Constance Talmadge, Arthur Johnson, Robert Harron, Mack Sennett, Lionel Barrymore, Henry Walthall, Owen Moore, Richard Barthelmess, and so on. For a long time the public knew their faces but not their names, and then the names became world famous.

The Biograph management was very strict on film saving, allowing about seven to eight hundred feet a picture, therefore no *two* cameras could be used at the same time—except in an emergency, like Mabel Normand's high dive in *A Squaw's Love*. Later, as pictures grew longer, we could use more than one cameraman, and it was up to the cutter to select the best shots. Jimmy Smith, and later his wife, Rose, were cutters par excellence and could be trusted to preserve the real meat of the nut.

All Griffith pictures after 1913 were made with a Pathé camera, including *Intolerance* and *The Birth of a Nation*. First, this was the cheapest camera procurable, and second I found it more to my liking. I could build things with it, such as wash-drawing effects, which were originated by me and afterward copied by other cameramen with more elegant cameras. In those days camera-builders and lens-makers never put anything in front of a lens. Until recently, even Kodak cameras had no sun shield on the front of the lens.

Zeiss, the German optical firm, built a special lens for me later, when I had enough money to afford it. I called it my *LG* lens, because I never used it except for special photography of Lillian Gish. I carried it with me, carefully nested in my vest pocket, as I considered it a most precious possession.

Another way we learned was through tryouts. Tryouts were usually in remote theaters, and it was to our advantage to be there. One memorable tryout was held in a converted store in the Lower East Side Jewish section of Manhattan. It was in 1912 for *The Musketeers of Pig Alley*, an early gangster film with Elmer Booth, much of which was filmed in that locale. We got very strong and favorable reactions—it was one of the first "realistic" films, one of our best.

At the tryout of another picture, there were several laughs which puzzled us at the time. We simply could not see what was so funny, but the audience could. We finally realized that, in a chase scene, an actor's clothing had become disarrayed and every time he turned a little off to the side, the tail of his shirt was hanging out the front of his pants. At least I knew it was his shirt; evidently the audience didn't.

Interrupting or cutting into a scene was not only new but daring, raising a lot of objections. It was criticized by our office most of all. To *make them look*, Mr. Griffith found that he had to bring the camera right up to the principal action, excluding all else for a time. This brought the audience, even the rear seats, closer to the action. The attendance at movies grew, and so did our popularity. As usual, the front office was convinced by the box-office receipts.

It was the stupidity of the front office that finally made Mr. Griffith come to the conclusion that he'd have to depart from Biograph. Like me, he was not by nature the changing type,

and he would have stayed there forever if they had only con-
ceded a few demands, which they had to do anyway after he
left, because that was the path movies were taking. The most
important thing was that he wanted to make longer and longer
pictures, but both Henry Marvin and J. J. Kennedy believed
the public would not be able to sit through longer pictures. In
1911, when he wanted to make a two-reel Civil War picture,
they made him break it into separate parts, *His Trust* and *His
Trust Fulfilled*. People went to see both parts and it did well
at the box office, but they still didn't get the message. That
same year we made *Enoch Arden* in two reels, and this, too,
was a success.

By the end of 1912, the popularity of movies throughout
America was obvious to everyone. Biograph pictures were the
best to be seen, and D. W. Griffith was the best director in the
business, though his name was still not known to the general
public, any more than those of the actors. He was approached
by other companies, starting with Adam Kessel, but he did not
yet want to give up the security and front-rank position of
Biograph. Addie Kessel settled for next best and wooed Mack
Sennett away from us to make comedies. Sennett left in the
summer of 1912 and took with him Mabel Normand and Fred
Mace, and also Ford Sterling, who had just begun to appear in
Biograph comedies. We were now vacating the Fourteenth
Street studio for a modern uptown building at 175th Street in
the Bronx. Then in 1913 Mr. Griffith decided to make bigger
and better films.

In California we started on *The Massacre*, a super-Western
that ended with only a baby's hand waving amid the slain bodies. It was a famous movie in its day. By the time we were
making plans for *Judith of Bethulia*, an epic in four reels, Mr.

Griffith told me he would not sign a new contract with Biograph.

"A film without a message is just a waste of time," he declared, as he paced the floor of my workshop, trying to convince himself, as well as me, that he needed to leave Biograph if he was to advance. "We are just grinding out sausages, Billy, and will continue to do so as long as we remain here. After five years, I think I have a right to my own vision, without being overruled by a lot of dunderheads in the front office."

"What's the answer, Mr. Griffith? We know what we have here, but I'm not so sure I'm ready to leave this old Rock of Gibraltar," I said. "What makes you so sure that other pastures will be greener?"

"For one thing, Harry Aitken. He's been making pictures for Mutual Films, and he's a good solid man. He believes in me and has promised to give me a free hand if I sign with him. I want you on camera, if you'll only come. We have a chance to make it big." He stopped pacing and faced me. "I wish you would join me. You will be glad you did, once you break away from here. You deserve a better deal than the one they have been handing out to you. Why, with all your years at Biograph, from the very start, you should own it by now!"

"Now wait a minute," I started to rationalize. "You're the one who's dissatisfied, not me!" As usual I didn't get very far. He had touched a sore spot: I was in a rut which would lead nowhere. Where other cameramen had forged ahead and grown rich in the process, I was just a member of the anonymous Biograph staff. They called me an "ace cameraman," but I never even had a contract. The money Nora had put aside was much less than it would have been if the pay had been more lucrative. I had never been in it for the money, and I was sure I never would be rich.

In October 1913 Mr. Griffith resigned from the Biograph staff and signed with Harry Aitken's Reliance-Majestic. In December I, too, resigned and agreed to go with him. Practically every one of the Biograph players went with us. From December 1913 to March 1914, we photographed in five reels *The Battle of the Sexes* with Owen Moore, Lillian Gish, Fay Tincher, Donald Crisp, and Robert Harron. We had already photographed the principal scenes of *The Escape*, based on Paul Armstrong's play, with Blanche Sweet, Mae Marsh, Robert Harron, and Owen Moore in the new studio in a loft building not far from Union Square. *The Escape* was not released by Aitken until June 1914. We were going out to California. Mr. Griffith knew what he wanted to do—a big Civil War picture *in twelve reels*.

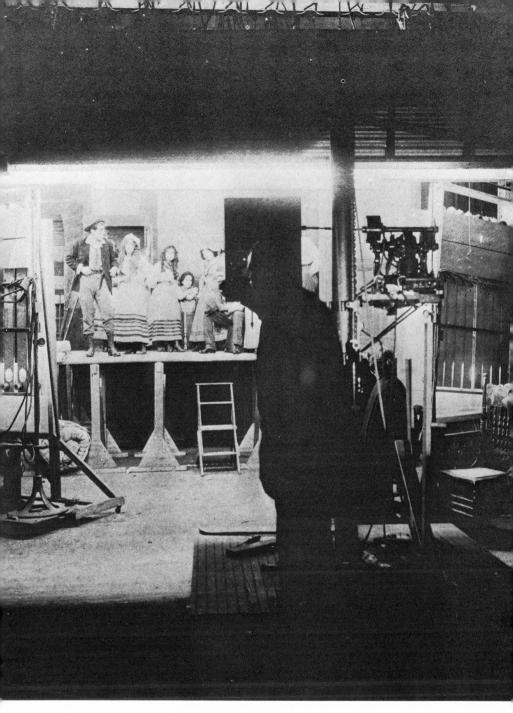

Rare interior shot of the Fourteenth Street studio in 1905, with Bitzer behind the camera. The film is unidentified

A Bitzer shot from *The Hero of Liao-Yang*, a film about the Russo-Japanese War made in 1904 in the Japanese garden of St. John's Military Academy, Manlius, New York

A Bitzer shot from *The Black Hand*, filmed on New York streets in 1906. Note bystanders watching the "kidnapping" of a child

A Bitzer close-up of pet guinea pig in *The Lost Child*, made in 1904 in Brooklyn

Exterior of 11 East Fourteenth Street, to which Biograph moved its studio in 1903

FORM NO. 1218   BULLETIN No. 68, May 16, 1906

SAN FRANCISCO

The Only Complete Moving Picture Production Showing the Fire in Progress

THE CONFLAGRATION AT ITS HEIGHT

A historic "news happening" filmed by Bitzer, the San Francisco earthquake and fire, 1906

FORM NO. 1322   BULLETIN No. 148. RELEASED June 80, 1908

AT THE FRENCH BALL

An Excruciatingly Funny Comedy of Errors

LENGTH, 670 FEET.   **PRICE, 14 CENTS PER FOOT.**

Before starting his directing career at Biograph, D. W. Griffith acted in several films, including *At the French Ball* (June 1908). The Bitzer photo, reproduced in the Biograph bulletin, shows Griffith wearing a clown's costume

THE MUSIC MASTER

A Most Beautiful Motion Picture Fantasy

LENGTH, 500 FEET.   PRICE, 14 CENTS PER FOOT.

A Bitzer shot from *A Calamitous Elopement* (August 1908), the first film directed by Griffith which was also photographed by Bitzer. This scene was filmed in front of 11 East Fourteenth Street, with Griffith playing the bit part of a policeman

Bitzer was behind the camera of *The Music Master* (May 1908), in which Griffith acted the title role, above left. Bitzer also used the indirect lighting of the fireplace for his self-portrait, below left

Rare photo of the first Biograph studio in California in 1910, with buildings still under construction. Bitzer, wearing light vest and soft hat, is the man nearest the camera. Griffith, with his back to camera, is the man on the stage in the dark suit

A posed shot of Bitzer at the camera and Griffith directing *The Avenging Conscience* (1913). Henry Walthall is the desperate phone caller

Another posed shot of Bitzer and Griffith examining a strip of film on the set of *The Avenging Conscience*

One of Bitzer's favorite stills, with highlighting in back of the actor, Wilfred Lucas

NINE

The Birth of a Nation

1914–1915

I was reluctant to leave New York for good, but when the time came for the move to California, I began to feel more and more excited about our big new venture. Garrulous by nature, I went about broadcasting the good news, hitting all my newspaper friends at their offices and visiting the "beach" in front of the Palace Theater on Broadway, where actors congregated in those days. They listened avidly to my stories; this was show-biz news. I was behaving the same at the studio, until one day Mr. Griffith took me aside and cautioned me to slow down. My talk, he said, would only stir up resentment.

This stunned me. He said it was true that he had many admirers, but human nature being what it is, others envied him and hoped he would destroy himself. As for business affairs, the simple truth was that we were operating on a shoestring. Griffith said he was almost broke; Aitken and Mutual (the distributor) had very little money. We were raising some through "quickies" like *The Battle of the Sexes*. He said we would have to hock Christy Cabanne's picture *The Great Leap* to pay the fares of the company to the West Coast. Now I understood why my bragging and boasting were so ill-advised.

"After we make good, you won't have to give out information, Billy," he said. "They will seek you out for the news. And we *will* make good." I had never seen him so determined and self-confident. Somehow, feeling the strength of his conviction, the fact that we were low in funds temporarily did not seem to matter. I believed in the man Griffith, and so did everyone else in the company.

Soon we were traveling westward on the Santa Fe Railroad, taking turns riding on the rear platform when it was not too dusty, playing cards, watching the scenery, and enjoying the trip.

"*Oh the days are so long and the nights have no ending, but we will be happy, dear, when the summer comes again,*" Griffith gave forth in song in his fine bass voice.

"Amen to that," said Kate Bruce, our elderly spinster, who practically lived on a diet of milk and played the perennial sweet mother. We finally arrived in Los Angeles, where accommodations had been booked at the Alexandria Hotel.

Our new studio consisted of a few bungalows amid a tract of fig trees at Sunset Boulevard and Gower. One bungalow for the office, another for my cameras, and one in which the Thoren family, who owned the property, lived. A large barn sufficed for dressing rooms and indoor stage. A platform was being set up in the yard for an outdoor stage.

At least three new independent companies working in and around Los Angeles sent word welcoming us and offering any help we might need. After all, we were now an independent company too. The three were the Lubin company, located in a two-story frame house with a small front porch and platform stage in the back yard, where they made "society" pictures with Harold Lockwood and Dorothy Davenport. Jimmie Youngdeer was another independent, making Westerns that were released through Pathé Frères. Deer, as he was called by the players, was an Indian married to Princess Red Wing, an accomplished actress who played alternating roles in his films, as did Miss Jackie Saunders and Louise Glaum. The third group, the company of William Selig, the first Hollywood pioneer, had their studio two long blocks away from the end of the Edendale car line. They used assorted players, but animals were their featured attraction. The snakes had been defanged and the lions' claws and teeth extracted; the animals were well fed and easy to work with, if you could put up with the foul breath of the lions. Kathleen Williams was the gorgeous redheaded Selig girl, and Hobart Bosworth, former star, was now the director.

In Hollywood there was this vast space to cover to get even a glass of beer. I had to keep my workshop bungalow well stocked with the stuff or go without. The best place for all-around sociability and good companions was Jim Jeffries's saloon in Los Angeles, the only bar around with swinging doors like we had back East. Jim and I were old friends, dating back to the time I filmed his fight at Coney Island. To me, at this stage, California left much to be desired—the land where the flowers had no perfume and the women no virtue. The Los Angeles River was a thin trickle of water, reminding us all that this had once been desert. The sewerage was bad and when it rained the whole area of Los Angeles would be flooded. The tap water was full of alkali, and you drank only the water sold in large tanks and delivered to your door. I was having trouble washing prints, and we had to erect a water tower for pressure on what we did use. My test prints came out badly and had to be sent to New York for processing. I sweated, fumed, cursed, and chawed the end of my stogie.

The eucalyptus trees, which had been brought here from far-off Australia to give shade, gave none. Their bark peeled and hung listlessly. Then there was the palm tree, which gave no shade or moisture, and looked listless and enervated if you were unfortunate enough to have one near your bedroom window, as I did. The pepper tree was forever shedding its crimson berries, which made the walks bloodred when you trod on them. A sameness of climate prevailed, except after sundown, when the cold winds came from the mountains and a sweater or a coat was needed. We found there was a grapevine of information being passed around by telephone operators who listened in to our phone calls, especially on long distance, where some rare morsel of conversation would be retold as a juicy bit of gossip for the neighbors, or even at times sold to the scandal sheets, which were becoming more bold and popular. The cliché "Who do you love today?" caused many reputations to be ruined by practical jokers. Tragic endings to several talented actors' careers were instigated by gossiping phone operators. Mr. Griffith cautioned us to deport ourselves extra carefully, for this was a small town, more dangerous than the city.

Right from the first, Griffith changed his directorial personality entirely. Where heretofore he was wont to refer to films as sausages, he now seemed to say, "We have something worthwhile and valuable in this drama of the Civil War." I could see and feel his eagerness. At first I thought the big price offered for the story—ten thousand dollars—to Thomas Dixon, the author of *The Clansman*, was crazy. Personally I did not share his enthusiasm, having skimmed through the book. I figured that a crazed Negro chasing a white girl-child was just another sausage after all. I was from Yankee country and to me the K.K.K. was sillier than the Mack Sennett comedy chases. A group of horsemen in white sheets? Preposterous. I was wrong again. Horror fascinates people and suspense gets them. You must have horror and suspense, and a ride to the rescue, if you want to hold the audience's interest.

When you stand alongside another man, day in and day out, as I did—with Griffith generally sitting right in front of me and the camera—you get to think you know his every emotion and mood. For example, I learned that his wriggling his foot as he sat with crossed legs meant "Not so good," even before the scene was finished. When he read a telegram from New York saying a certain picture was below par, he would usually start singing, to let off steam built up from frustration. *"Save your money, for the winter time is coming soon"* was his favorite song to fit this occasion.

"You get that old camera of yours to photograph this right, Billy," he would say, "and we won't be eating at Childs any more. We'll give them pictures that will blow off the tops of their heads."

His strong point was never a sense of humor, though occasionally his face would light up with a smile. Yes, he often smiled, but I never remember hearing him really laugh.

In July, we started shooting *The Clansman* (it didn't become *The Birth of a Nation* until just before the New York opening). There was no night photography, of course, and it was all done by sunlight, even the assassination of President Lincoln in Ford's Theater. The carpenter-made model-miniature of the burning of Atlanta, which had to have special lighting to make it look real, was the only scene I can recall that we did not shoot by sunlight.

This was not just another picture for Griffith. He was fighting the old war all over again and, like a true Southerner, trying to win it or at least to justify losing it. Old Colonel "Jake" Griffith had schooled his son well with yarns of his fighting days. As we followed the story—there was no written script, it was all in Griffith's head—this passion consumed him. He *lived* every minute of it, blaming the carpetbaggers for seeking to profit from the South's sufferings and glorifying the clansmen for rescuing those fair flowers of the South, Elsie Stoneman (Lillian Gish) and Flora Cameron (Mae Marsh).

In the battle scenes of *The Birth*, which we did first, Mr. Griffith directed practically single-handed. I was cameraman for the entire picture and shot every foot of it, though I had help from my assistant, Karl Brown, who was then in his teens. He wanted to learn about cameras and he certainly did, becoming one of the best in the business and a fine director, too.

For mob scenes we used hundreds of extras, who were organized in groups under leaders like George Siegmann, Elmer Clifton, Erich von Stroheim, Raoul Walsh, Christy Cabanne, and others. We had no loudspeaker system then. Griffith used a megaphone and it wasn't always easy to hear a command. For the battle scenes, the units were assigned numbers for firing shots, and we had to be careful because each volley of our precious blanks cost money.

Here I was down in a ditch with my camera, shooting the

horses and wagons as they passed overhead in battle action. Or I would be photographing the men in the trenches who were firing their guns straight at me. The fireworks men would be exploding smoke bombs in the camera range, and often the wind blew so much smoke in my eyes I could hardly see what I was doing.

"Lower, lower," D.W. would shout to the fireworks men through his inadequate megaphone. "Can't you get those damn smoke bombs lower?"

My legs were pitted with powder burns already, but all that mattered was that the bombs were coming up within camera range. Turning the crank to three-quarter waltz time—first with one arm and (when there was a break in action and a chance to change over) then with the other—that's what I was there to do. Those turns had to be absolutely constant, the same rate of speed over and over, but the rhythm was so much a part of me that I felt I could do it in my sleep.

In filming Sherman's march to the sea, we needed cannons and had arranged to get some from the artillery corps stationed in Los Angeles. The crew bringing them out to Universal Field was held up, and while we were waiting, Griffith noticed a family group on the hill nearby. At his direction, I inched the camera unobtrusively up to them, all the while pretending we were after shots of the valley below. Later, the combined scenes, edited by Jimmy and Rose Smith, would vary the long panorama shot with this little intimate picture of a mother and her children caught in the grip of war. It was one of the touches that made *The Birth* so real and convincing to audiences accustomed to stilted acting and stock shots, especially in costume movies.

The horses in this film were almost as important as the actors. For one thing, it was mid-1914, war had broken out in Europe, and horses were in great demand. We had managed to get some high-class steeplechase jumpers with riders from a local race track; they were fine animals and expert horsemen. When they came charging head-on, it was so thrilling I almost forgot they were on camera. Griffith asked one of the riders if he could jump into the air, leaping over my camera. I was afraid the camera would be wrecked, so we tried it with me prone on my stomach, underneath the jump, and it worked. D.W. then decided to try the same device for the ride of the clansmen. The trouble was that these riders were not so expert as the jumpers. Also, they were swathed in white sheets and hoods, with only eyeholes to see through. In addition, the horses were hooded in white in the same fashion. Wally Walthall, the "Little Colonel" of the story, was an expert rider, and his horse leaped over me with no trouble, except that a cloud of dust blinded the follow-up.

"If they come too close, I can roll out of the way," I yelled to Griffith. Scores of horses were now stampeding past me and swerved to the sides as they saw my camera. But one rider had had to dismount, and the long sheet had blown over the horse's head, blinding it momentarily as it rushed ahead. Griffith ran out, seized the reins of the frightened horse, and nearly had his arms pulled out before he stopped the beast and calmed it down. Fortunately for me, he had a way with horses; he even picked out the horse to play "Traveller," Robert E. Lee's horse. It had to be just the right dappled gray. You'd think we were back in 1864–5. Of course, in Griffith's mind we were.

D.W. acted as if the budget we were supposed to follow did not exist. As the cost of production mounted, the home office in New York sent frantic wires to Griffith. When their investment reached $78,000, an alarming sum, they felt they never would get any of it back.

Each morning at seven-thirty I would pick Griffith up in the company chauffeured car at the Alexandria Hotel. It was only a ten- or fifteen-minute ride to our studio and we had a chance to talk relaxed. One morning I looked for him in the lobby, where he usually waited, but he was nowhere in sight. I asked at the desk and found he hadn't come down yet. I then went up to his room and knocked on the door.

"Come in, Billy," he greeted me. He was shadowboxing and went right on with his exercises as though I wasn't there. I took a seat, watching the action.

"Read that telegram on my night table," he said bitterly. "The damned fools!"

I picked up the wire and this is what I read: WE WILL SEND NO MORE MONEY. FINISH PICTURE IMMEDIATELY.

"Well, Mr. Griffith," I said, "you better do as they say."

"I will like hell!" he raised his voice. "I'm not inclined to quit now, or any other time."

"But what will you use for money?" I asked.

"I'll get around that all righty, all righty." He paused and looked straight at me. "Have you any money socked away, Billy?"

"I have a little, not much though."

"Maybe enough for the people today—four hundred?" he asked.

I had a thousand dollars stashed away for emergencies. This must be one.

"I guess so."

"Well, let's go get it then!" he said, grasping my hand firmly.

On the way to the studio, we stopped off at my savings bank, where I drew out four hundred dollars. This would cover the payroll for the day, he said, for the extras only, $385.00. The principal actors would have to wait.

My friend George Siegmann was in charge of the extras. When the day's work was done, he went to the pay office, as usual, to get the money. J. C. Epping, our treasurer, told him to come to me for it. This was his first cause for alarm. The big fellow came to me with a grin on his face.

"Well," he said, "don't tell me our precious cameraman has turned angel?"

"Cut it out," I told him. "I'm just tiding us over until Griffith finishes the picture. There's been a tie-up, but the money will be coming from New York any day now. It really isn't much."

"It isn't much! What do you mean? You're a bigger chump than I thought. Can't you see the handwriting on the wall, Bitzer? This guy's digging his own grave." Then he returned to the business at hand. "Where's the dough?"

Next day I went back to the bank and drew out the balance—$600. The next day, and for many days thereafter, I drew from Nora's and my joint account in New York. It soon mounted until I had drawn $7,000 in all. I was forced, reluctantly, to tell Griffith beforehand what my limit was, and he was able to find another angel. It was some mysterious woman, known only as That Woman. I never learned who she was. Her share in *The Birth* was $9,000. The next to give cash was Bill Clune, of Clune's Theaters, who put up $15,000.

Our costumes were being furnished by the Goldberg Company, which now wanted to be paid. When Mr. Goldberg found he could not get cash, he was persuaded to take payment in stock. His bill for costumes came to $7,000, and like me he made much more from the stock than he would have from cash.

When *The Birth* was ready for preview showing in Los Angeles, we used the twelve original reels. The audience reaction was very good, but Griffith still felt we could use more footage. As there was only one camera—mine—shooting the entire production, it is well he did. *The Birth* was taken on the hand-cranked $300 Pathé camera with a 2.52-inch lens interchangeable and a wide-angle lens; you had to screw it out and screw the other into its place. The old projector had long been outmoded, and the new projectors were much too rapid, so every inch of film was used at some time or other. With time, the prints wore thin from repeated duplicates taken from the original negative and the pace was lickety-split on the screen.

Ten years after the first showing, Mr. Aitken, who still owned *The Birth*, consulted me, and I deemed it best we insert film twins—two identical picture frames coupled where one had been. Thereby we doubled the original twelve reels to feed into the new, more rapid projector. This was successful.

The Birth of a Nation opened at the Liberty Theater, New York, in March 1915, at two dollars top. Such a price was unheard of for a motion picture. Prior to that time, when it was previewed at a special showing as *The Clansman*, Thomas Dixon suggested the title be changed to *The Birth of a Nation*, which proved to be wise and was accepted.

The picture cost $110,000, a tremendous figure in those days. The original budget had called for $40,000—also an unusual sum for a movie.

Sensing my money worries, Griffith assured me I would be

one of the first to reap the rewards. I left for New York to be on hand for that possibility. Opening night found me out in front of the theater, watching every dollar that came into the box office. I'd never seen anything like this sale of tickets.

I returned three or four times, watching the long lines forming in front of the box office. As the days went by, they kept getting longer and longer, and finally stretched halfway around the block. I knew my investment was safe and would pay me dividends beyond my wildest dreams. Over the years *The Birth* grossed $20,000,000 from all its showings. From the day this picture opened, the movies became big business.

Griffith had his younger brother, Albert Grey Griffith, help him in the management of finances. To lessen the name confusion, Albert dropped the Griffith and thereafter was known as Albert Grey. There were mutterings of internal strife on the financial or dividend side. Just what they were, I never knew. I was getting my end of the profits each week, anywhere from twenty-eight to thirty-five hundred, and I cared little about the bickering going on.

I found, however, that the eyes of the entire moving-picture world were upon us. Everyone wanted to make pictures like *The Birth*. My services as cameraman were much in demand and I could name my own price, but I decided to stand with D.W. Harry Aitken had the controlling hand in our several studio operations. His eye fell upon me idling my time away back in Hollywood, waiting for D.W.'s return, before we got started shooting in earnest again on the big new Babylonian picture.

"Say, Billy," Aitken suggested, "how'd you like to direct a flier for a change, until D.W. gets started again? He might be away a long time. I'll pay you one grand a week, with a bonus if you finish in less than the three weeks the schedule calls for." The picture was to feature Olive Thomas, a Ziegfeld Follies girl, who later became the first wife of Mary Pickford's spoiled brother, Jack. Although the offer intrigued me, I suspected a strong undercurrent motive to separate me from D.W. I decided to stall for time. I took several test shots of Miss Thomas to ascertain her photographic propensities. She had beauty, but she was a type new to me—arrogant, brassy, and curt to the point of being rude.

I needed the advice Griffith could give, so I phoned him. "Don't do it, Billy," Griffith cautioned, over long-distance phone. "If you fail at this, your first big attempt, your reputation as a winner will be destroyed. I'm not returning under the old banner. I have big things coming up for us, so take it easy. By the way—this is important—if and when you leave, be sure to take *The Birth* negative with you." This conversation left me in a quandary. But one thing kept nagging at me; "When you leave, be sure to take *The Birth* negative with you." As there was only one such, its possession meant nine-tenths of the law. Though Griffith's decision was not quite according to Hoyle, I knew there must be a legitimate and necessary reason behind it.

Even before Griffith warned me that Miss Thomas could not act, I was skeptical of her ability. From the very first rehearsal, she showed a lack of seriousness and any semblance of concentration. I should have stopped right there, but there was *The Birth* negative in the vault to consider. My chance to get it loose came unexpectedly. Miss Thomas and I had to go to the costumers in Los Angeles, and on the way we passed the Alexandria Hotel. She suddenly decided to stop and refresh herself with a champagne cocktail. I objected. She ordered the car stopped and made off without me. I followed, however, joined her at the bar, and had one cocktail. (She was well ahead of me.) Then I asked her to leave.

"Another drink wouldn't be bad, Billy," she replied.

"Listen, if you don't do as I say and come along, there'll be no picture. Either you come, or we're through." She knew I meant it.

Her friend Miss Cassidy joined us at this point. "Don't let that big slob tell you what you can or can't do. Order your drink."

Turning to me, Miss Thomas said, "Go soak your head!"

I left to figure out my next move and do some scheming about the negative I needed. How was I going to get possession of it without the knowledge of others? I went back to the studio and took Joe Aller into my confidence. He was a young man I had advanced from apprentice to laboratory chief. Explaining that Griffith wanted *The Birth* negative put in some safe place until his return, I told him I would take it now, just in case someone else had different ideas. I warned him of the necessity of keeping this secret.

The next morning I took the negative to my bank and placed it in a safe-deposit box. When D.W. arrived in Hollywood, I turned it over to him. Why he needed it or what he did with it, he never told me. However, his troubles with the money people seemed to be straightened out. First Mr. Aitken announced the Triangle group—D. W. Griffith, Thomas Ince, and Mack Sennett—and then he formed a company for our new film, *Intolerance*, within the Triangle organization. Griffith was very happy when our new name was announced, the Wark Producing Company.

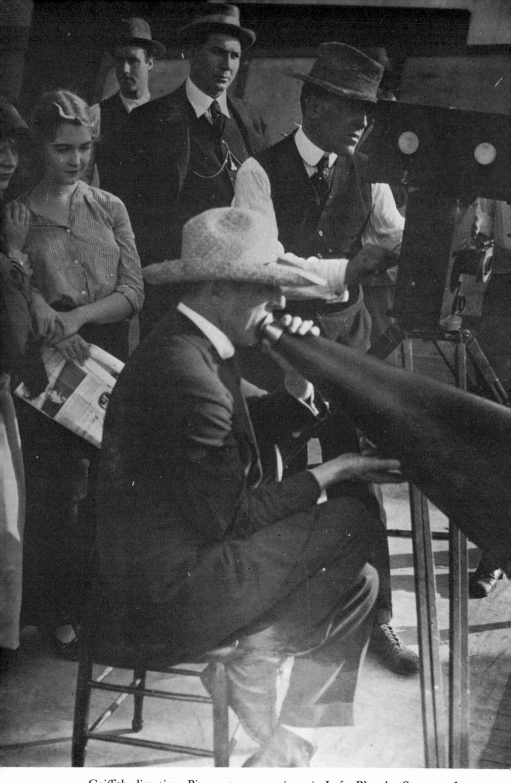

Griffith directing, Bitzer at camera (1914). Left, Blanche Sweet and
Dorothy Gish; rear, Howard Gaye; right, Karl Brown

Sherman's army marching through Georgia in *The Birth of a Nation*. The house shown in the upper photo is burning in the lower one. The next three pages are battlefield shots by Bitzer

The Birth of a Nation: Henry Walthall as the "Little Colonel," above. Josephine Crowell, Lillian Gish, and Walthall, below

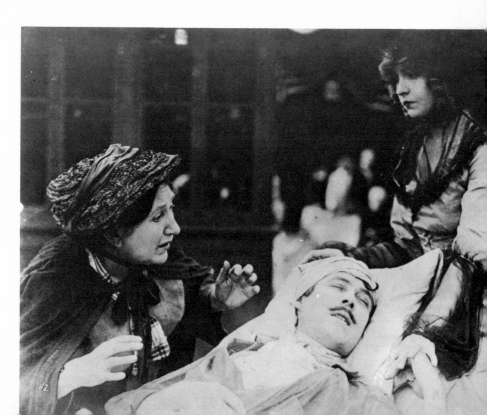

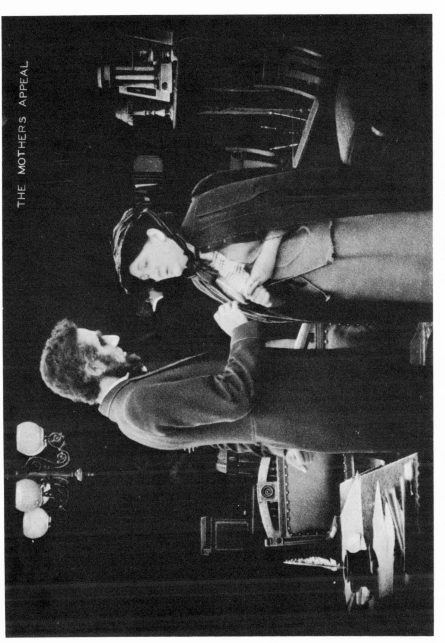

THE MOTHER'S APPEAL

Josephine Crowell intercedes with Lincoln (Joseph Henabery) for her son

Signing the Emancipation Proclamation, above. Below, Robert E. Lee (Howard Gaye) surrenders to U. S. Grant (Donald Crisp)

The ride of the Ku Klux Klan. The ladies are Miriam Cooper and
Lillian Gish

Griffith (in white suit) on the set of Ford's Theater, before the filming of Lincoln's assassination (opposite page). Note use of natural light

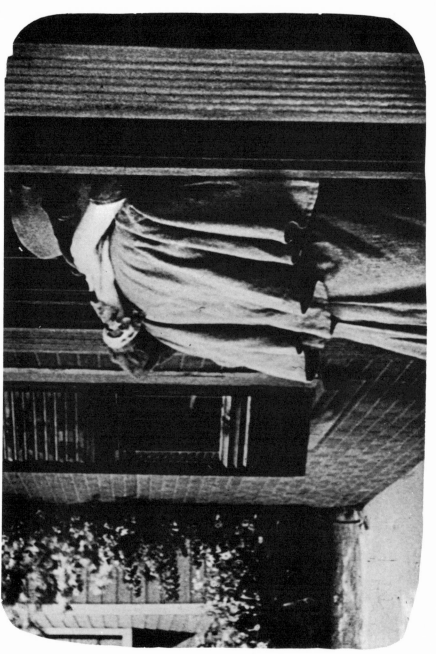

Bitzer's famous homecoming shot of the "Little Colonel"

A Bitzer composition: Lillian Gish and Henry Walthall in *The Birth of a Nation*

--❦ TEN ❦--

Intolerance

1916

We had completed another film before we started on *The Birth*. It was *The Mother and the Law*, a modern story of the wrongs inflicted on working-class people, with Bobby Harron and Mae Marsh both giving great performances. I was hoping Griffith would release it, because I thought it one of our best. But he now wanted to top *The Birth*, which all the writers hailed as the greatest picture yet made, and was thinking of doing another Babylonian story, a spectacle like *Judith of Bethulia*. In fact, with the success of the ride of the clansmen in mind, he asked me whether I thought I could get some of the same effects with a herd of elephants. I said, "Mr. Griffith, where would we get the elephants?" We couldn't get them, of course, with wartime shipping troubles, but he got them in the picture anyway—they figure as stand-up sculptures on top of the walls of Babylon.

Mr. Griffith wasn't satisfied that the Babylon story would

be enough by itself. He was smarting from the charges of racial prejudice that were made against *The Birth*, and he even wrote a little book, *The Rise and Fall of Free Speech in America*, to tell his side of the story. He was hell-bent to answer his critics with the greatest movie ever made on this theme—intolerance. Griffith now had more money than he ever dreamed of, and he finally decided to weave together four separate stories of bigotry, in four periods of history, and tell them simultaneously. He'd begin with the modern story of a strike, "The Mother and the Law." Then he'd go back to early history and show the fall of Babylon, laid low by the Persians.

Then what? Well, there was the age-old intolerance meted out to the Jews. For information on the Hebrew episode, Griffith was referred to a rabbi living in Los Angeles. D.W. spent considerable time with Rabbi Myers and got to know his family, including the rabbi's beautiful daughter Carmel, who was allowed by her father to act in the picture, the start of her career. All the details of the Jewish wedding at Cana were approved by Rabbi Myers, as were the costumes and the sets for the entire Judean sequence. The fourth historical episode chosen by Griffith was the religious persecution of the Huguenots in France, ending in the massacre on Saint Bartholomew's Eve. There was one final touch, involving Lillian Gish, which I'll explain later.

The little lot in California, corner of Sunset and Hollywood Boulevard, had boasted just a couple of platforms and a few sheds used by the Nestor independent company before we added what we already occupied with our Fine Arts units. When we finished *The Birth*, we were still terribly cramped and needed more space. Bit by bit, we encroached on the Thorens' (our adjoining neighbors) property, by renting privileges of first one patch and then another. We finally coveted the only area left. On this ground were a hundred or more of Mrs. Thoren's small fig trees, her pride and joy. All the persuasion of the entire executive staff was of no avail. We were walled in and needed that fig-tree space to keep back the curious street mobs from getting into our scenes. At one point it became so important that there was talk of offering Mrs. Thoren a percentage interest to change her mind. Suddenly she decided, for some sentimental reason, to let us purchase the land.

Huck Wortman, who had charge of the construction of the big sets in *Intolerance*, was a rough sort of down-to-earth fellow who chewed tobacco incessantly and spat out of the corner of his mouth. In the original laying out of these sets, working without a scenario (there were no paper plans), Mr. Griffith, Huck, and myself would go over on the adjoining field and stake out where D.W. thought he would like to have them, my end being their relation to the sun—lights and shadows. (The actual shooting was to take place on the larger sets some six to eight months later, so the sun's position had to be considered.)

These sets kept growing larger and higher than the original staked-out areas, as Mr. Griffith kept asking Huck, "Could we put another wing on here or increase the height there?" Huck generally agreed, and many a night before bedtime when Huck or I would hear a Santa Ana windstorm getting strong, we would jump into our cars and, with a couple of men Huck always had ready, go to the *Intolerance* lot and add a cable here and there, and tighten up the others. Huck would kind of look at Mr. Griffith when another twenty-foot-or-so higher part was suggested, but he never rebelled.

HUCK WORTMAN WHO HAD CHARGE OF THE CONSTRUCTION OR
~~THE CONSTRUCTION~~ OF THE BIG SETS IN |INTOLERANCE| WAS A
ROUGH SORT OF DOWN TO EARTH TYPE OF FELLOW. CHEWED
TOBACCO INCESSANTLY, ~~...~~ AND SPAT OUT OF THE CORNER OF
HIS MOUTH. IN THE ORIGINAL LAYING OUT OF THESE SETS, LIKE
MR. GRIFFITH WORKING WITHOUT SCENARIO THERE WERE NO ON
PAPER PLANS (AS OF TODAY) MR. GRIFFITH., HUCK, AND MYSELF,
WOULD GO OVER ON THE ADJOINING FIELD, AND STAKE OUT. WHERE
MR. GRIFFITH, THOUGHT HE WOULD LIKE TO HAVE THEM. MY END
BEING THEIR RELATION. TO THE SUN, LIGHTS AND SHADOWS. THE
ACTUAL SHOOTING WAS TO TAKE PLACE, SOME SIX AND EIGHT
MONTHS LATER. SO ON THE LARGER SETS SUNS POSITION HAD TO BE CONSIDERED.
THESE SETS KEPT GROWING LARGER AND HIGHER THAN THE ORIGINAL
STAKED OUT AREAS. AS MR. GRIFFITH. KEPT ASKING HUCK. COULD WE
PUT ANOTHER WING ON HERE OR INCREASE HEIGHT THERE. HUCK
GENERALLY AGREED AND MANY A NIGHT WHEN BEFORE
BEDTIME HUCK OR I WOULD HEAR A SANTA ANNA WIND
STORM GETTING STRONG WE WOULD JUMP INTO OUR CARS
AND WITH A COUPLE OF MEN. HUCK ALWAYS HAD READY /
GO TO THE INTOLERANCE LOT AND ADD A CABLE HERE,
AND THERE, AND TIGHTEN UP OTHERS. HUCK AT TIMES
WOULD KIND OF LOOK AT MR. GRIFFITH AT TIMES WHEN ANOTHER
TWENTY FOOT OR SO HIGHER. PART WAS SUGGESTED BUT HE
NEVER REBELLED, ONE MORNING AS I WAS COMING ON THE
LOT AND HUCK STOOD IN A SORT IN OF MENACING WAY. AS I
WAS COMING TOWARDS HIM (AT TIMES I CARRIED ADDITIONAL OVER
NIGHT INSTRUCTIONS FROM MR. GRIFFITH, TO HIM.
cont

Reproduction of a page of Bitzer's handwritten manuscript; see edited
text, opposite page

One morning Huck stood in a sort of menacing way as I was coming toward him (at times I carried additional overnight instructions from Mr. Griffith), and it occurred to me to kid him a little. As I came up, he said, "What's it now?" I said, "Oh, on those side battle walls, would it be much trouble to put runways and have platforms for horses and chariots?" With a "Well, I'll be—! What will he want next?" he just stood there. A little later, when Mr. Griffith arrived, Huck asked him, "How many horses and so on do you figure putting on them walls?" Mr. Griffith thought a moment and said, "Say, Billy, that would be a good idea. Would there be too much vibration for your camera?" The horses and chariots are up there in the picture.

Huck would say to later stupendous construction suggestions, such as the 110-foot-high moving camera dolly, "This ain't a-going to be another horses-and-chariot gag, is it?"

One of Huck's great designs was the big, heavy gates of Babylon, which were opened by slaves pushing big iron wheels on either side of the gates. That set with the walls is the most sumptuous affair we ever attempted. It was 150 feet high, not 500 feet, as given out in publicity.

The reason we had to have the camera dolly was that the balloon, which we tried first, did not work. I had to get the entire set in full view—a real bird's-eye view—from the air, then zoom downward gradually to the dancing Virgins of the Sacred Fires on the steps, then zoom into the big banquet hall, for many yards, and finally pinpoint a little toy chariot, drawn by two white turtledoves, as it moved across the floor with a love letter from Belshazzar (Alfred Paget) to the Princess Beloved (Seena Owen). Now remember that the whole set was about three-eighths of a mile long and that I had to start suspended in the air 150 feet high. When we tried it first in the balloon, the trouble was that the basket rocked, the horizon kept changing, and I began to get seasick. I thought that if my camera did not fall out, I would. But Huck Wortman worked it all out fine with his next construction. The dolly was 150 feet high, about six feet square at the top and sixty feet wide at the bottom. It was mounted on six sets of four-wheeled railroad-car trucks and had an elevator in the center. This dolly ran on tracks starting way back and taking in the entire set, on which five thousand extras were assembled, including lines of standees across the top frame of the set.

This great dolly was moved backward and forward by manpower; twenty-five workers pushed it smoothly along the rails. Another staff operated the elevator, which had to descend at a regular rhythm as the railroad car moved forward. The whole scene had to be filmed in one continuous shot, in focus at every level. It wasn't easy to do. We rehearsed it over and over.

It was shot with only one hand-cranked Pathé camera. Karl Brown, seated underneath the Pathé, did the cranking through a flexible shaft. I handled the tilt and pan cranks, looking directly through the Pathé eyepiece focusing glass in the back door of the Pathé onto the film, with a special eyepiece of rubber, which fitted around my eye, to keep the light from fogging the film. It was a brilliant sunny day, and the whole thing came out fine and clear.

Huck Wortman was a peach, just another one that adored Mr. Griffith. The Babylonian set still holds the record for being the largest ever constructed for a Hollywood production. It remained standing until the 1930's, and Griffith tried to get Hollywood to put up the money to preserve it as a movie-industry landmark, but down it came. When we finished the feast of Belshazzar, Huck Wortman said to me, "There won't be one in fifty people that see it will know what it's all about!" Then to me, "Do you?" And in honesty I had to say to Huck, "No."

One day D.W. entered my bungalow. "Billy," he said, "when you were a boy, did you go to Sunday school?"

"I sure did, Mr. Griffith. My first crush was on my Sunday-school teacher."

"Well then, you must know 'While shepherds watched their flocks by night, all seated on the ground,' " he began.

"I know it well. 'The angel of the Lord came down, and glory shone around.' "

"And the last verse, Billy, goes, 'Thus spake the seraph, and forthwith appeared a shining throng of angels praising God.' That's what I want, Billy. Angels in the sky overhanging the cannons of the battlefield. Peace triumphant over war—it's going to be our epilogue."

"Great, Mr. Griffith. How many angels do you want?"

"Oh, let's say not more than a hundred. Just enough to fill the picture."

I went to the property department. "Get costumes for angels. Make it about seventy-five."

"But, Mr. Bitzer, that's an awful lot of angels. Must he have that many?" The head property man took the pencil from behind his ear and wrote something on a pad, then went away muttering to himself, but I was certain we would get the angels.

Mrs. Brown, our wardrobe woman, made the long white gowns with wings. As the angels had to be suspended in the air, she also made belts of burlap binding, as used under chairs to keep the springs in place. She tried out one girl as a model.

I went over to Huck, poor overworked man, and asked him to erect stout poles in the yard and get some cable wire. It was no sooner said than done. He got about thirty telephone poles that cost sixty dollars each. I told him to place them far enough apart in the lot so they would be out of the camera angle.

As they were bringing them in and unloading, old eagle-eye Griffith espied them, forgetting what he had asked for.

"Stop those damn fools from putting up those telephone poles," he said to me.

"Don't worry, Mr. Griffith, they are only temporary. I need them for the angels."

"Angels?" he said, mystified. "What angels?"

"Why, don't you remember—the angels you wanted to fly in the sky over the battlefield."

"Oh, yes. Of course. Yes. I was thinking of something else." He began to get that look of the dreamer, muttering to himself, "Maybe Mars, the war god, would be better. We'll see."

Sixty girls were hired as angels. They looked real cute in their gowns, each young face prettier than the next. Then Mrs. Brown's burlap belts were adjusted under the gowns. Then the wire was hooked to the belt and we tried it out. Much depended upon that flimsy wire. On some girls, the belt pulled up to just under the arms, and on others it slipped. We pulled them up slowly, and they squealed and spun around like crazy. First thing we knew, a few were fainting, others vomiting, and half were brought down and revived. I thought we would have more dead angels than dead soldiers in the scene.

We cajoled some of the sick ones into trying it once more,

and got some replacements. More money, more wires, more work. We adjusted their belts so they would not circle around or spin. Placing a man under each angel with a control wire not only lessened their movements but gave the girls confidence. With my camera on the runway, I was able to move under them. It did not get the effect of flying very well.

We were on it all day. It was briefly doubled in over the battle action, in the big Armageddon scene of the epilogue, predicting the bombing of New York and the destruction of the world if men did not achieve universal peace. All that work with the angels ended up a ten-foot flash. What Mr. Griffith saw in his mind we put on the screen.

I sent for my brother Carl, who had some camera experience, telling him that now was a good time to come out to Hollywood and get into the swim. I also sent word to my sister Anna's boy Lou, to come and be my assistant cameraman, for he was strong, twenty-six, and over six feet tall.

We rented a ten-room bungalow, furnished, on Canyon Drive, so we could all live together temporarily. Carl and his wife, Mary, came with their two sons, Jerome and Paul, livening things up a bit, especially for me as I loved children. Mary and Nora, both Irish, disliked each other from the very beginning. There was much squabbling in the kitchen until I decided to hire a maid, who couldn't get on with either of them and promptly left. Regardless of appearances, it was Nora's kitchen, and she didn't mean to relinquish it. When Nora got back her kitchen, I hired Tony, a Mexican houseboy, who besides doing housework could drive a car; so I bought a Packard. Tony, in turn, talked me into buying an Oldsmobile racing car, which he was forever getting new parts for to get the speed up to seventy-five miles per hour. This became my boastful pride and joy.

The bungalow we lived in was offered, furnished, for $12,000. I wouldn't buy it, for I did not expect to live in California. As an investment, I figured it would be worthless as soon as we movie people left. Wrong again. Instead we went right on renting at $125 a month.

There truly were many exacting rehearsal requirements during the large set scenes of *Intolerance* that would have taxed the strength of several men, but Griffith sat in on them all. Raoul Walsh, who acted John Wilkes Booth in *The Birth*, was one of D.W.'s assistant directors. He would sometimes take over during long repetitive rehearsals, when D.W. would just get up and walk away, leaving Raoul in charge while he disappeared for a while. Before I learned different, I imagined he went to the office to discuss finances. I should have known, had I given it much thought, that it wasn't about money, for he never was one to worry about cost. One day I followed and found him in his office, lying on a couch, relaxing and figuring out the mechanics of the next scene. He was really giving the actors a chance to get together and develop a mood or attitude for the scene. With him away, they could relax and do it their own way, more naturally.

At luncheon, especially on location, he would eat alone and concentrate on his notes for the afternoon shooting; then he would put the notes away, which allowed him freedom of motion. When he had the action running smooth, he would send for me and rehearse before the camera, so that I could get the lighting and movement just right. During the final rehearsals, I would get my scratch pad out, together with an old silver stopwatch I carried in my vest pocket for the purpose of timing the scene. The cast usually knew the rehearsals were over when he said, "Get Billy, and we will time it now."

Griffith's messenger had trouble finding me one time. I was goofing off some place with a bottle of beer and good company, so I grabbed my scratch pad, but forgot my vest with the stopwatch in the pocket. I had to go back for it, causing an added delay. From the set to my bungalow took about fifteen minutes of our time so, while waiting, Griffith ordered someone to go to downtown Los Angeles and buy me a wristwatch. Few men wore them then, but he had been given one by an admirer and he recommended I get one too, but I thought it too sissified and was afraid I might come in contact with something electric and get a shock. Within an hour, Griffith handed it to me by strapping it on my wrist. I was forced to wear it all day, but at night when I got home, I put it back in its case and left it there. He had taken my old pocket watch to make certain I would be forced to wear the wristwatch until I got used to it, at least. I never liked wearing any sort of jewelry and tried to get my old watch back by inquiring around where he had put it, but it was gone.

The next timing rehearsal, I had no timepiece. Grabbing a darkroom timing clock, which ticks out the seconds, I placed it on the floor away from Griffith. In one of the quiet moments of rehearsal, he started looking around, and I was sure he had heard the ticking even before he asked Raoul, "Is there a clock around here some place? I hear ticking."

"Yes, Billy has a clock on the floor beside him." Raoul grinned in amusement.

"Of course," Griffith defended me and went on with rehearsal. "Sounds good."

As the nights were long, quiet, and cool, the urge to work after sundown grew strong. After all the heat and sweat making *The Birth*, it seemed the reasonable thing to do. But how to capture the strong light needed? Griffith kept turning this over in his mind and wished for night shooting. Inquiring around, he decided to risk it, shooting with klieg lights and flares. Then he invited the other studios to participate, bringing their own cameramen, directors, and electricians who could study its merits. They came and were convinced. Step by step, they argued the benefits and costs of such a venture. One by one, the studios accepted the idea and put it to use, but the extras wouldn't buy it and challenged it. They expected additional overtime recompense. They were referred to J. C. Epping in our treasury department, and he was furious over their demands. He paid, however, because Mr. Griffith said he had to. "Take care of this, Epping, it's infinitesimal but pressing."

On the first night, Mrs. Lee, who had the lunchroom across the street from the studio, was given an order for five hundred sandwiches and several gallons of coffee. She handled most of our business, and usually made up ham and beef sandwiches, so she did the same for this Thursday night. It was fifteen minutes before midnight when the food arrived. As soon as it was spotted, down came the thundering herd of extras. A brawny Irish Catholic, who had a host of followers, started an outcry against the meat, for he could eat no meat after twelve o'clock. If you were a Catholic, you did not eat meat on Friday. With but fifteen minutes to go, they made short shrift of the five hundred sandwiches, well before midnight.

The story of the sandwiches made good reading for the local papers, but it created a new problem. At night people would watch the sky for night-light reflections, jump into their tin Lizzies, and ride toward the lights, hoping they could catch the making of a movie and free eats. Then the stores and markets stole the idea of using lights for their openings, hoping in that way to attract business to their shops. Next it was movie houses, using it for their premières. The skies of Hollywood were no longer star-studded by night; the movie stars had taken over.

Howard Gaye, an English actor who had the role of Robert E. Lee in *The Birth*, was excellent, and Griffith wanted to use him again. He was tall and slender, with a long serious face, graceful hands, and a smooth carriage. Griffith cast him as the Nazarene, and he made a most convincing and appealing Christ.

Griffith was constantly warning the players to keep in character during the making of his pictures, but during *Intolerance* our switchboard was alive with protests from the old families of Hollywood. While still in the costume robes, with beard and long flowing hair, Howard Gaye would hop into his Ford and ride around Hollywood, ogling the young girls.

"Imagine, Christ riding down Hollywood Boulevard in a Ford!" the old natives screamed in protest.

As Howard behaved well around the lot and never bothered our young girls, we thought he must be cautioned against leaving the lot in costume. He explained to Griffith he was only trying to shock the blue-nosed natives and gave us no more trouble. Shortly after leaving us, he formed his own company with money he had saved from his earnings. Young girls came to him for parts in his pictures. One fourteen-year-old made charges against him, true or false, and he was deported to England. When these damaging charges were sub-

stantiated, his name was taken off the screen credits for
Intolerance.

Constance Talmadge played the mountain girl who worshipped Belshazzar from afar. She was truly the wild unruly
tomboy she portrayed. She palled around with Dorothy Gish,
another tomboy. Connie was made to order for the part. Her
big scene was to squat on a stool, while milking a goat. "Come
on, Connie, get the milk," Griffith urged. The goat veered
away, turned, then gave Connie a most provocative warning
glare. Putting forward her head in imitation of the lady goat,
Connie moved toward the challenge. Then their heads col-
lided with a bang. We had all of this on film, and it remained
that way in the picture. "You all right, Connie?" Griffith
asked. "I think so, Mr. Griffith, but it hurt. Do I have to do it
over again?" "No," Griffith said with a grin. "I don't think
the goat wants to play any more. You're too rough."

So many things happened during the months of making
Intolerance, it would be impossible to recall them all. We
were happy and without the constant financial worries so familiar to us all.

But if my studio life was happy, my home life was anything
but. Nora was experiencing the changes and acting oddly.
There were those violent fits of temper which preceded her
love affair with the bottle. There was constant fighting with
my brother's wife over money, and it ended in their sudden
departure for New York, leaving the house empty. My only
regret was having sent for them.

Then Nora begged me, with promises of reform, to send
for her sister Kate's daughter, which I did, and with it came
the first serious threat to our home. It wasn't long before I
had Maysie Redford in the group of the famed Ruth St. Denis

dancing girls in the Babylon feast scene. Since we were to-gether many hours of the day, it wasn't long before I learned to love this younger version of Nora. However, Maysie didn't feel the same about me, for I was only her dear Uncle Billy. She, in turn, fell in love with Raoul Walsh. He, in turn, fell in love with Miriam Cooper. It was all mixed up and crazy.

Blond Seena Owen played the Princess Beloved, adored by Belshazzar. Seena was a truly beautiful girl, who needed no help from the camera. For a time Griffith had been undecided whether to use her in such an important part, or Alma Rubens, who was dark. He gave it to Seena and I thought he made an excellent choice, for Seena was exquisite. What worried Grif-fith was Seena's weight problem, something the camera could not hide. We were sixteen months making *Intolerance,* and he was fearful she would outgrow the part. Always one to keep his players on edge, he noticed that Seena, like all the rest of the susceptible females, was enamored of George Walsh, Raoul's brother. George was an outstanding athlete, a great swordsman long before Fairbanks, and when he came West to visit his older brother Raoul, Griffith immediately signed him for the part of the groom at the wedding feast of Cana, be-cause of his dark, handsome face. Griffith, in a friendly chat with George, dwelt on Seena's feminine beauty and kind na-ture. George listened, susceptible to the flattering confidence bestowed on him. Griffith next had a friendly chat with Seena, and soon we noticed the pair together, happy with their new-found love.

When a call from the wardrobe department later relayed the information that Seena was putting on weight, Griffith called in George: "I think I've been wrong about Seena. I should never have put her in the picture as the Princess Beloved, she's too fat!" To Seena he said, "You're wasting your time on George, he's merely using you. He's not the marrying type and he's having too much fun to settle down. He indicated that in our conversations. Don't worry, you're better off without him." They became estranged. I'd see Seena slowly walking in front of the studio after hours, waiting for George. Griffith purposely was keeping them apart by sending George off the set when she was working. The strain began to show, and Seena lost weight.

Before finishing with our Babylon sets, we used flaming arrows and sheets of flame for the scenes of Cyrus's siege of Babylon. This was left for last, as we might inadvertently destroy part of the set. An ever watchful Hollywood became alarmed about what we were doing. Fearing for their property and what could happen to that dry open land, they gathered together in protest and decided the best thing to do was call the fire department.

Unsuspecting, we went ahead with shooting the scene. We had everything as we wanted it and the scene was going off perfectly when out of nowhere the fire apparatus came charging up the side road which we had fenced off, right to the big gate, with orders to the gatemen to open up. What seemed like the entire Los Angeles fire department rushed in.

Griffith sprang to life as though shot from a cannon. With tact and diplomacy, he convinced the chief we had everything under control, we would soon be finished, there was no cause for alarm. Getting rid of them before our elaborate sets could be ruined and a great deal lost presented quite a problem, but he did it.

Bessie Love was the bride and George Walsh the groom in

the story of the wedding feast at Cana of Galilee, where Christ turned water into wine, the first miracle. By the time this was filmed, on a set away from all but those concerned, Seena had completed her assignment and returned East with a broken heart. George, on his part, revealed a wild side to his nature which troubled his brother. Raoul wisely waited until the picture was in the cans before confronting his younger brother. I understand they had a heated argument, ending in George's declaring his love for Seena. "Go after her, George!" Raoul advised, and George went, and they were married. Shortly thereafter Raoul took his own good advice about settling down and married Miriam Cooper.

Lillian Gish was given a part no one envied. She had been a star in *The Birth* and was resting on her laurels. Now she was cast as the hand which rocks the cradle of life eternal. Quote: "Endlessly rocks the cradle, uniter of Here and Hereafter." Griffith wanted this to be symbolic of endless time, connecting his four stories. The shot appeared five or six times throughout the picture. It gave me the opportunity to develop my new *LG* lens, especially built for me by Zeiss-Tessar. All Lillian need do was sit and let me worry about making her beautiful. This business of rocking that old cradle spoiled the picture somewhat, for people could not understand it.

Lillian was ever without emotional show. Griffith conditioned her to the part she was to play, and once she had the action in mind, she wouldn't forget or deviate by so much as a flicker of the eye. Her interpretation would be as directed, without waste of precious film; standing immobile, her face expressionless, in deep concentration until she heard the call "Action!" She was our first thin woman. She was around sixteen when she came to us with her younger sister, Dorothy. She had pale blue eyes and a clinging-vine appeal. Her seeming helplessness took everyone off guard, covering up her inner strength. Her hobby at that time was collecting watches. To me Lillian spoke of her few tiny watches or of the poems she had read which her idol, Griffith, had recommended. Her adoration of him was no secret and never had been.

I had to put a halo light behind her hair to get that angelic look. She would stand or sit so long without moving, waiting for the signal. As I never could get a subject to be so patient, I began to get some very beautiful effects with her. In the end her patience and ladylike behavior were rewarded.

Opportunity often comes to the patient, for after Mary Pickford we had several other girls playing top roles. Beautiful Blanche Sweet was one, and lovely Mae Marsh was another. But it was Lillian Gish who patiently waited the time out to become Griffith's best-known star player. *The Birth* was her first big success, but it took *Broken Blossoms*, a sleeper, to bring the artist in Lillian before the public. After that she was universally acclaimed as a star.

Mae Marsh was one of my favorite performers. Mildred Marsh had been with the New York company, when one day her elfin sister Mae crashed the set. She came popping out at us from every corner, grinning like a Cheshire cat. The spirited child in Mae caught Griffith's fancy, and the battle was won. In making her a player, he had another pawn to use in the game of working one against the other, his real stock-in-trade. "If you don't think you can do this part justice, say the word, and I'll get Mae to do it." This was enough to bring on the jitters and set their adrenalin flowing.

Mae's freckled face and friendly manner were contagious.

I put her brother Ollie Marsh on as camera assistant as soon as
he was big enough to carry a camera. He was bright and hard-
working. He stayed in California after we left for New York,
and rose to be a master cameraman and one of the founders
of the American Society of Cinematographers. It was at Mae's
behest that I put him on, and it was a pleasure to do her a
favor.

A Bitzer still of Seena Owen in *Intolerance*

The walls of Babylon, *Intolerance*

The Persians scaling the walls. An assistant director in shirt sleeves
(right corner, top) got into the frame by mistake

A Bitzer still of the slave market, with the auctioneer and customers at left. Madame Seldawan (grandmother of Dorothy Dandridge) displays the slave

Inside Babylon's gates, resisting the enemy with flame throwers

Filming *Intolerance* at night

Lou Bitzer, Billy's nephew, measures his six feet two inches against the towering height of Ishtar, goddess of love

One of Bitzer's greatest shots: Belshazzar's feast. Note the statue of
Ishtar, right center, in proportion to the whole set

Constance Talmadge, as the Mountain Girl, in *Intolerance*

Belshazzar (Alfred Paget) learns that Babylon has fallen

The Persians at the gates of Babylon

Howard Gaye as the Christ in the Judaean sequence of *Intolerance*

A Bitzer still, the gates of Galilee

The marriage feast at Cana. Lillian Langdon is Mary, the mother of Christ; the bride (Bessie Love) and bridegroom (George Walsh) are under the canopy

The stoning of the woman taken in adultery, above. The prince of peace, opposite

The way of the cross

Catherine de Médicis (Josephine Crowell) and her sons, from the French sequence of *Intolerance*

Above, triumphant procession of Charles IX. Right, the Duc d'Anjou (J. A. Beranger) in trouble

The massacre of St. Bartholomew's Eve, *Intolerance*

The modern story: their infant is restored to Mae Marsh and Robert Harron, center; Tom Wilson stands in background

The society social worker throws a modest party, *Intolerance*

Workers leaving factory, *Intolerance*

The police raid a house of prostitution, *Intolerance*

American types at soda fountain (Mae Marsh second from left), *Intolerance*

Shooting the racing-car rescue scene in *Intolerance*. Griffith at left, Bitzer behind camera. Opposite page, directing an outdoor scene; the man at right front is Frank Woods, production supervisor

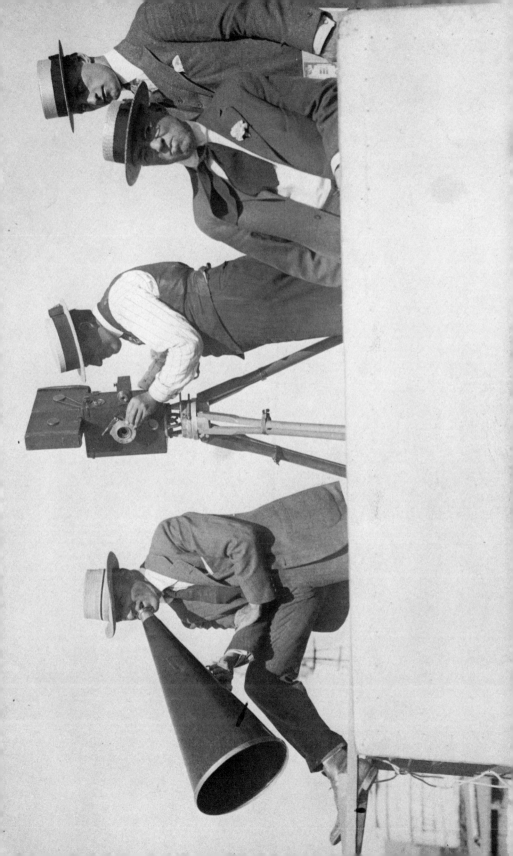

Griffith, Bitzer, and Woods on the set

Bitzer with Mae Marsh, one of his favorite actresses

ELEVEN

Hearts of the World
1917—1918

Early in 1917, Griffith sailed for England. He was tired and felt dried out from the exhausting hours spent on *The Birth* and *Intolerance*, both of which were being shown successfully in London. England and France were fighting a hard war with Germany and needed help; naturally they looked to the United States, but Woodrow Wilson and the whole country wanted to stay out of it. It would take much propaganda to succeed in enlisting our aid. Prime Minister Lloyd George of England consulted with his allies. Neither a book nor a play could reach enough people in this emergency, but a motion picture . . . D. W. Griffith, the world's foremost director, was the *one* man who could tell a story that all—Americans especially —would understand. In London a group of VIP's called on Griffith at the Savoy Hotel, where he had taken up residence. They laid out their plans before him and pressed him into accepting. Then he was invited to meet the Prime Minister at

No. 10 Downing Street. Then, in April 1917, the United States declared war against Germany, but it was decided to make the film anyway. Griffith sent at once for Lillian Gish and her mother.

I was back in Hollywood, waiting to hear from Griffith, who, I thought, would soon be back in harness in California. Otherwise I would have accepted outside offers, for I disliked being idle. Added to that was an unhappy home life. Nora was out of touch with life, lonely for the past, and felt her usefulness had come to an end. Her smile was sardonic, her tongue was bitter, she quarreled with Maysie Redford and sent her back to New York. The doctor wanted Nora to take the Keeley cure. She would have to go away for the treatment and was terror-stricken at the prospect, so I hadn't the heart to force the issue. She begged for just one more chance and I couldn't refuse.

Then came D.W.'s cablegram from overseas; he had been commissioned by the Allies to make a war propaganda picture. My instructions were to come at once and bring Dorothy Gish and Bobby Harron with me. I directed all serious thought to putting things in order in case of my non-return. First, I gave away my jewelry—the diamond ring Mary Pickford had given me, the gold wristwatch Griffith had given me, another gold pocket watch from the camera staff, a pearl stickpin—they all represented some epoch in my career. As for friends with whom I had invested money for their enterprises, I now turned over full ownership. The rest of the money, stocks, and bonds I left to Nora without reservation.

Then I conceived the idea of burying gold, in case by the time I should return proper money would be worthless. I got $1,200 in twenty-dollar gold pieces, which was easy to do in

1917. In the still of the night, after I was certain all in the household were asleep, I slipped out into the back yard of our Canyon Drive bungalow and dug a deep hole under the apricot tree in our hen yard. Here I buried the gold in a cigarette carton as a precaution against future need.

I gave my faithful nephew, Lou Bitzer, instructions that were to be followed in my absence, which he accepted as his duty and responsibility. He had great sympathy and affection for Nora, and tried to help all he could to keep us together. He played the piano very well and could improvise, on the spur of the moment, any tune he heard. Because of his good nature and willingness, I was sure all would be well in my absence. Our houseboy, Tony, would stay on to do the chores.

True to her word, Nora was once more a good wife. Always an excellent cook, she now surpassed herself. Only once did she step out of order, and that was understandable. With the declaration of war came many slanderous remarks about the Germans, and my Germanic name was bandied about by one of our neighbors, with Nora coming to my defense. As this was the first time in my life I was ever attacked, it came to me as a big surprise.

When it came time to go, I collected Dorothy Gish and Bobby Harron, and we left for New York. After we embarked on the *Baltic*, we were surprised to find we were sailing with General John Pershing and 385 officers of the A.E.F. We had not been apprised of the general's presence until after the ship was loaded with auto trucks, called lorries by the British, which covered every inch of the fore and aft decks. There were only six non-military passengers besides ourselves. We sailed at dusk and had got out a little way this side of Sandy Hook when the engine stopped, a Coney Island boat came alongside, and the high-ranking officers came aboard.

I had the whacky notion I would rather have been on one of our transports, which sailed in groups accompanied by destroyers. Here was a lone ship, with no convoy scouring the sea for a periscope, carrying the cream of our army personnel —a prime target. However, nothing of importance occurred, except an alarm for the ship's drill. The purser had not assigned me to the same lifeboat as Bobby and Dorothy, so when the *Baltic* let off three blasts of her siren, I awoke Bobby in our cabin and we rushed to Dorothy's cabin on a different deck. Dorothy was in such a state of trembling collapse she set Bobby to shaking too, and I was not much better. We rushed through the corridors to the lifeboat deck, where I finally got Dorothy and Bobby into their life jackets; then I had to get into mine. I was just in time to hear an officer finish the roll call: "Johann Gottlob Wilhelm Bitzer! Johann Gottlob Wilhelm Bitzer is missing!" On board ship I was no longer Billy Bitzer, but the name which appeared on my birth and baptism certificate. I was embarrassed and Dorothy started to giggle, but after I made my presence known to the officer at my station, all became quiet again.

During the voyage I did get to photograph General Pershing on the deck and took another picture of him on our arrival at Liverpool. I also got some fine pictures of his reception at the dock. How badly they needed American aid was displayed in that cheering welcome. In my excitement, I just walked off the ship, taking pictures and mixing with the crowd. When I tried to get back on board, I was promptly arrested and charged with violating the alien labor law. Then I was cleared through my papers, which showed the nature of the mission I was on. However, they went through my luggage, and some fifty packs of little American White Owls were opened to see if I had any secrets in there. Then a heavy tax was levied on them.

As they were my favorite cigars, I just had to pay the fine. My feelings for the English were not improved. This was to change shortly, for they are a wonderful people.

Everything had been arranged for our stay at the Savoy Hotel. Dorothy joined Lillian and her mother, Griffith as usual shared a room with no one, while Bobby and I occupied a large room with bath. The windows were heavily draped, so no particle of light could be seen outside, in case of air raids. The bathroom was a real delight, for it was large enough to work in comfortably, and the tub would do for my developing and all the rest which goes with the photographer's end of the game. But now it was just a tub to bathe in. While Bobby was unpacking his things, I bathed, washed my hair, and shaved. Then it was Bobby's turn.

Bobby had never weighed much, but now as he stood at the washstand combing his hair, wearing only an undershirt and shorts, his toothpick legs and skinny arms amused me.

"Does it hurt to be so thin, Bobby?"

"If you're going to criticize, how about yourself?" He puffed out his cheeks in imitation of my round face. "You old pumpkin head."

We spent our first night gathered together in Griffith's room, making plans for immediate production. Next morning found me up early, as usual, for I had to go over to Eastman's for film. It was about eight blocks from the Savoy and I wanted the exercise, so I walked. It was a clear day, but I saw no one on the street. Within two blocks I heard the call: "Take cover!" I stood like a stray dog, in the center of the street, because I saw them—the planes! Like flashes of silver fish they came into view and then disappeared again in the sky. I heard a noise like the crackle of lightning. As yet I was unaware of fear, so I finished walking to Eastman's, for now it seemed to me the danger was over. When I entered the shop, there wasn't a soul to be seen. Then from the basement a man's voice called to me: "For God's sake, man, close that door and come down in the basement until the all-clear signal is given!" I scurried down to safety with him.

Shortly the all clear sounded, and I walked back to the hotel. With the two cans of film I had picked up at Eastman's under my arm, I scanned each face I saw and spotted a man who looked like an American, for he had his hands in his pockets. I took a second look and recognized an old friend, Lowell Thomas.

"Lowell, what're you doing here?" I called out.

"Billy Bitzer! I'm here taking pictures, same's you. It's darn hard to get film, Billy. I see you have a couple of cans under your arm, where'd you get it?"

"Eastman's," I told him. "We can have all the film we need because we're doing a propaganda film for the English government. Use my name and they'll give it to you, or you come see me at the Savoy." The next time I saw him was at the British Press Dinner at the Savoy; he said he now had plenty of film.

Back at the Savoy I found Lillian, Dorothy, Mrs. Gish, and Bobby. They were highly excited because when the sound of bombing was over, they had gone up on the roof of the hotel and were just in time to see the German raiders returning from their missions. Dorothy explained excitedly that she had seen the enemy pilots leaning over the sides of the planes, smiling down and waving at the watchers on the roof. There was no danger, for the raiders had used their bombs and their mission was over.

Lillian suggested that we see just what damage, if any, had

been done, so we got into a car driven by a lady chauffeur and hastened to the spot that had been hit, in the poor section of town. A bomb had been fired on a school, and the children and teachers were the victims. It was here that the first realization of the horror of air raids finally penetrated through to us. When you hear the moans of the dying and see their mangled bodies, you realize what war is all about. We left the rubble and thought by getting to work immediately we might forget this scene. But we never did.

In filming *Hearts of the World*, we worked mostly out in the country on location, and it would be late when we returned. As a cameraman's work is never finished with the day's shooting, I would hasten to our room and develop the day's work. Film itself has a very disagreeable odor if you are not used to it; added to that was the disagreeable smell of the developing fluid, which Bobby disliked. There wasn't much I could do to remedy the situation.

While all London's surrounding countryside is very beautiful and charming, I think one of the most picturesque spots must be Lady Churchill's estate. It was here that I photographed England's most beautiful women—Lady Lavery, Lady Diana Manners, Elizabeth Asquith, the Countess of Massarene, Princess Monaco, the Countess of Drogheda, and Bettina Stuart-Wortley, who had volunteered as extras. Queen Mother Alexandra, old and not too strong, also came to be of help. Some scenes were taken in the Army and Navy Hospital at Combe Hill. Divested of jewelry and elegant clothes, in the simple garb of nurses, the angelic beauties looked more beautiful. A photographer from Foulsham & Branfield was at hand to take still pictures for the press. The ladies had arrived in their usual rich clothes and jewels, wearing a fortune in pearls, which for some reason they handed to me. I put them in my coat pocket, where they soon became burdensome. The weight made me lopsided, so I took off my coat and hung it on a tree. There was such a class gap, one wondered at the complacence of the working class which supported them. The upper classes did the accepting while the poor groveled according to long-standing custom. From the careless manner in which these ladies handled their jewelry, I wondered if they were born with ropes of pearls around their necks and tiaras to play with. To them, as a photographer I was merely a working man, which I certainly was.

Griffith now sported a derby hat, winged collar, and bow tie. After this day of shooting on the Churchill estate, Griffith and the ladies took off, leaving me to pick up my outfit when I had filmed all the extra footage we would need to make duplicate sets back in Hollywood. The gardener, a nice old fellow, came over for a friendly chitchat, which he could not have done while we were working. I was curious about some markings I had seen around the tree boles; they looked like metal tags that had been removed recently. He showed me many silver nameplates that had been removed, and on examination I was amazed to read the names of German royalty. "I shall put them back when the war is over," he said. "The German and the English royal families are cousins." For all his years of service in the garden, he was straight as an arrow. I asked him if I could take his picture. "I would rather you didn't. They might not like it."

Going on location to bombed-out areas was reminiscent of my early "News Happenings" days, spent in emergency zones in which havoc had been wrought. Griffith had the use of a Rolls-Royce to carry the actors and himself to location. I used a taxi, for I had my camera, props, and light reflectors to think about. We had a prop wheelbarrow to carry, for it fit into the story. This I had tied to the luggage rack of the cab. I'm sure it looked better there than it would have on the Rolls.

As a bomb site once demolished is an unlikely target for a repeat attack, that was what we had chosen. This picture told the story of a small French village under German occupation. The actors—Lillian, Dorothy, and Bobby—stepped from the Rolls in make-up and costume. Dorothy, in her street-singer outfit with black bobbed wig, in the story worshipped Bobby from afar, while Bobby, nattily dressed and wearing a small mustache, was engaged to Lillian. Both girls are left behind in the village at the mercy of the Huns.

While it is true many scenes were made at the battle fronts in France by cameramen, I did not go there, and neither did any other member of the company, except Mr. Griffith. Our pictures of the front came from No. 10 Downing Street, after being approved by Prime Minister Lloyd George. Our lives were never in jeopardy from the continued bombing of England and France, and it was plain to see that the poor suffered most from the war in both places. War may enrich or impoverish a monarch, but he is clever enough to take none of the blame, and by the use of propaganda he justifies his moves. People never ask why the royal families never go to battle as of yore; instead they look about for some scapegoat to justify their frustrations. This is sometimes directed upon the so-called draft dodgers or other men in a non-combat status.

Bobby Harron became a victim of much of this abuse. Chafing under the scorn heaped on him by the ignorant, he wished to protest being called "Bloody draft dodger!" but was not allowed to, lest he incite riots.

Hearts of the World was really a Hollywood picture, invested with enough actual battle-front material and enough scenes taken over there with our American actors to make it seem real. More than half the footage used was shot in Hollywood. It was also one of the first propaganda pictures made with government sanction. It was not against war, but against defeat by the enemy, and I went along with that. The film was successful and got over its point, even though it was April 1918 by the time it was shown.

One evening Bobby had returned before me and was bathed and dressed when I came into the room with my camera and tripod, the reflectors, the wheelbarrow loaded with film cases, tins of negatives to be developed, and a lace headscarf I must dye for Lillian's love scene with Bobby. With the aid of an elderly porter, I had managed to bring it all up in the freight elevator. Bobby was edgy from the taunts of cowardice hurled at him during the day, and when he saw all the things I was bringing in, he just threw up his hands and fled the room.

A few weeks later there was a real blowup. I liked a bottle of beer while I worked in the evening and this was sometimes impossible to get, as the pubs closed at nine, so I gave instructions to the room valet to see I had two bottles in my room every day. He was to leave them in the tub, where they would be cool, for there was no ice. I was assured of that luxury, at least. Bobby didn't drink. On this occasion we had been out on location and did not get back for two weeks. We had said nothing at the hotel, as we did not know how long we would be away. On our return, Bobby went straight to our room. While I was busy bringing up my equipment, he sat reading a pile of mail he had received from home. When he finished, he said, "Now for a nice hot tub. Boy, could I just use it after all those dirt holes." As he made for the bathroom, he called out, "Hey, Billy, come here!"

In the tub were some twenty-eight bottles of beer, all piled up nice and neat. The valet had carried out my orders to the letter. I burst out laughing, but Bobby didn't see what was so funny about it.

"I'm getting tired of having the tub cluttered up with your junk. I never get a decent bath any more. The room smells of your cruddy film, and now this! Why don't you go drink some place else? I'm going to get another room by myself, even if I have to pay for it!"

"Oh, Bobby, don't get sore," I reasoned. "See, I'll take the beer out myself, it won't take but a minute."

"It isn't just the beer, it's everything. I'm sick of it all. If it wasn't so late, I'd move tonight."

"Well, as far as I'm concerned," I said, getting my temper up, "I'm sick of living with you, too. You keep the lights on late every night and never think that I have to work hard every day and get out earlier than you. I'd like to get some rest around here. Go ahead and move, that suits me just fine."

I emptied the tub of the troublesome beer, Bobby had his bath, and I had mine. When I entered the room, Bobby had extinguished the table light beside his bed. I lay there, unable to sleep from tension. We were both sorry for the harsh words we had exchanged, neither wanting to admit it.

Suddenly there was a sound like a gun. Bobby was the first to jump up and put on the night light. His thin face was white.

"Billy, did you hear something?" he asked in alarm.

"Yes, I thought I did."

Then there was another bang that sounded nearer. Then a whole series of shots were fired. I realized it was coming from the bathroom. I moved toward the bathroom with Bobby trailing. The floor was covered with white foam. It was the beer, which the heat from our baths must have set off.

It was all right between us from then on. We both gave in a little and did not annoy each other as before. The fight which had almost broken our friendship was over. Bobby began to understand me and my work, and extended a helping hand when he could, for which I was grateful.

We flew over to Le Bourget airport in France to get some aerial pictures. Although I was considered too valuable, insurance-wise, to do the actual shooting from the top of an airplane, nevertheless I had to set up my camera, get the focus, and give general directions for the official cinematographer who would take over from there. Climbing to the top of the plane, with only a vest to shield my shirt, I quickly set up focus.

"All right!" I shouted to the cameraman who would take my place. The French pilot understood it as his cue and promptly taxied off, while the official cameraman shouted helplessly. I was standing up on the wings, without straps, but the camera was firmly set up so I clung to it. I couldn't have let go if I had wanted to, for my hands were frozen to the camera crank. It was bitter cold and the wind was terrific. It seemed an eternity before the pilot realized his mistake and taxied back. I was all right as soon as I found the bottle of whiskey in my back pocket and took a swig.

We also took village scenes in the vicinity of Montreuil, three kilometers out of Paris. We chose this location, for it had once been the home of Pathé Frères studios, now closed and desolate from neglect and disuse. Close by was the shrine of Notre-Dame-des-Anges, where the peasants prayed for miracles, a scene which we used in *Hearts*.

Back in London, I went sightseeing again before I sailed home.

Lillian Gish and Robert Harron in *Hearts of the World*. Opposite, a publicity shot of the war wounded in a London hospital, with Lady Diana Manners and other society "nurses" grouped around Griffith

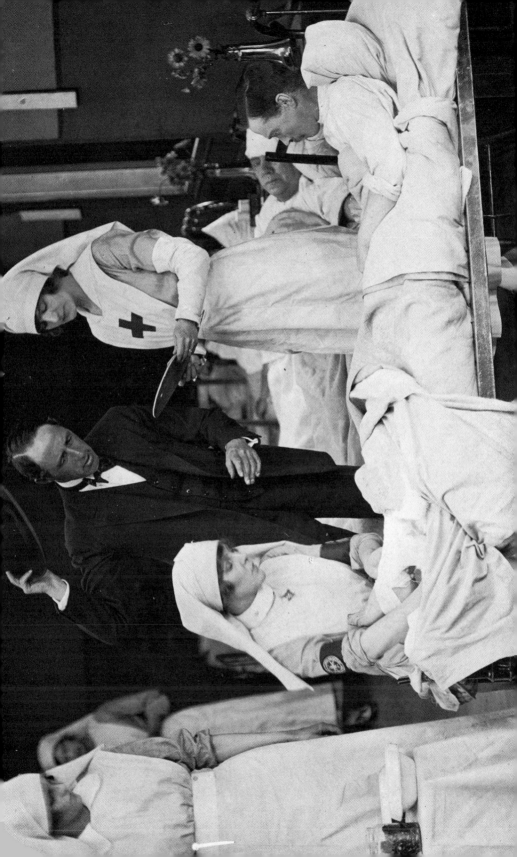

DAVID WARK GRIFFITH ON THE BATTLE-FIELDS of FRANCE

At British Field Headquarters

In a front line trench 50 yards from the Germans

Left, from Griffith's press album. Right, George Fawcett greets
Robert Harron at the front

Publicity shot in France: D. W. Griffith with English officers

⊶ TWELVE ⊷

Broken Blossoms

1919

Returning to the States from England, I stopped off long enough in New York to run up to the Griffith offices in the Longacre Building and was received warmly by the secretary Miss Conway and by Jack Lloyd when I picked up my checks. Then I ran over to *The New York Times* and chatted with Bosley Crowther, the movie editor; next I visited Roy Mc-Cardle of the *Morning Telegraph*. It was good publicity for our forthcoming *Hearts of the World*, which we would finish in Hollywood. After spending the night at the Claridge Hotel, I was off next day for Hollywood. Bobby Harron stayed on with the Griffith party, then came on with the Gish sisters and their mother. Griffith traveled alone.

Griffith had agreed to a legal separation from Linda, by mutual consent. I think he preferred it that way. He wanted no woman interfering with his daily commitments, film was his only love. It was a compulsive thing, hard to explain—you

197

can't stop. Linda, on her part, was in no hurry to remarry and avowed she would never consent to divorce. She would receive thirty thousand a year for as long as she lived. Money, as I have said, meant nothing to him. I visited Linda many times after their separation, and she was always open and candid with me. I had been in her confidence since the troubled days of Dorothy West. At that time I had been unwittingly made aware of her desperate heartbreak over losing him when the failure of their short-lived marriage put an end to her hopes. It was best they part, for she surely would have ended it all in tragedy. Keeping the marriage secret was his first strong weapon against her, something she should have wondered about many times. Then his insistence on living in separate abodes, which removed him from permanent home life, was another signal for her to grow wary. She never gave up the fight to hold him, and every new face loomed as a threat, real or imagined. Lately it was Lillian Gish, whom she personally disliked, who gave her anxious moments.

As the train neared Los Angeles, I began to wonder what my homecoming reception would be like. Although I had my work and all the money I needed, I was past forty and childless, except for the pathetic woman I called wife, who was worse off than me. What I had filled my life with was endless hours of concentrated work. All I thought of really was my camera. How fondly I regarded it can only be realized by some other camera-fiend. I kept it in the pink of condition at all times, never retiring for the night without running my fingers lovingly over it, looking for some real or imagined defect. My sole concern was that lovable/ugly camera, the Pathé. To take it from me would have hastened my demise.

I now go on record to blame myself for much that had happened to Nora. I had spoiled her normal life by taking her into the false world of make-believe and idleness. Perhaps I could make it up to her.

I was surprised to see my nephew Lou at the station. He looked well and cheerful. "Everything all right, Lou?" I asked suspiciously.

"Oh, sure. Aunt Elinore's fine," he answered easily.

"So it's Aunt Elinore now, is it? What happened to her old name of Nora?" I was curious about the change.

"Her real name is Elinore," he said. "Don't tell me you didn't know that."

We walked over to a new Pierce-Arrow in the parking lot. "What happened to the Packard?" I asked.

"Aunt Elinore sold it to a guy who is going to use it for a private taxi. Got a good price for it, too."

As Lou drove out to Hollywood, I noticed many changes along the way. For one thing, the Chamber of Commerce must have been at work: there was roadside latticing on El Camino Real in an attempt at rose-bordering, and there seemed to be more oil drills around, some even on the front lawns.

As we turned into Canyon Drive, I felt like the prodigal son at seeing his old home: "I found the house swept and decorated." I stepped from the car and approached the brown-shingled bungalow, which looked like Buckingham Palace to me. There were Japanese lanterns on the porch and an air of welcome around the house. Out stepped Nora, smartly dressed and charmingly healthy. She flew to my arms. "Good boy, Billy," she said over and over, and she couldn't say more, for welcoming tears had choked her voice. Soon we were surrounded on all sides by smiling neighbors come to greet me and welcome me home. They had planned a homecoming party for the evening, so there was much hustle and bustle about the premises.

I stepped out into the back yard to look around at the Japanese decorations. Then, with a gasp of disbelief, I hurried to the spot where I had buried my gold. The hen yard was gone! There stood an outdoor fireplace with a huge black kettle hung over charcoal embers.

"Do you like it, Uncle Billy?" Lou's voice broke in. "I built it myself. Aunt Elinore's cooking chili in that big pot. Took me two weeks. I had to tear down the fencing first."

"Nice work, Lou, but do you have any idea how far the fencing stuck out?"

"It went around the apricot tree, is that what you mean?" he reassured me. "This is more up to date. But if you want it the way it was, I'll put the fence back."

"Hell no, Lou. Leave it just as it is, and thanks." I remembered the apricot tree. The ground between the fireplace and the apricot tree was nicely lawned. Yes, I could see I would have no trouble retrieving my gold. I was back in the party mood.

Before a picture is cast, a search for new faces is made. Actors use still portraits, profile and full-face, an expensive investment in a hard-pressed profession, but it's the only way a producer can select casts without personally seeing the actor. A good still photographer helps.

So it was when Carol Dempster left her pictures with the casting department and Griffith thumbed through them. He was first intrigued by the photographer's skill; then he studied the face which seemed to come out of a new method of lighting. The photographer was Hendrik Sartov. Griffith sent for him, as well as the girl.

Sartov had made several revolutionary portraits of Carol at a Hollywood studio. He knew next to nothing about movie camera technique or running a motion-picture camera, but with my training, his new method could become a valuable property. Many of our boys were still in the army, so we needed all the talent we could surround ourselves with. One of my best assistants, Charlie Downs, had enlisted. Sartov was an apt pupil, foreign-born, with an accent and a resigned nature. What he had in talent, he lacked in enthusiasm: he always seemed bored. Later Griffith saw to it that we shared honors in credit for photography. Until now, I was the teacher and my assistants learned from me. Suddenly, with the entrance of Sartov, everything changed and I was the pupil, learning from him. Isn't that a gasser? That's show biz.

Soon after Sartov mastered the movie-camera technique, Griffith sent for Carol and had him make a test of her. Then we made tests of sundry actors for the lead in *The Chink and the Child*, as our next film was then called, before it became *Broken Blossoms*. Out of those tests Griffith selected Richard Barthelmess, who had done some excellent work in a war picture starring Alla Nazimova. This was a terrible blow to Bobby Harron. Griffith was happy with the new soft-focus photography and would use it in his next opus. Carol was fine as a Ruth St. Denis dancer, but she wasn't quite ready for a large dramatic role. He would use Lillian, who did not seem to want the part, if she could be made to look like a child of twelve. I made that test, and she did look half her age.

Incidentally, Ben Alexander had been tested by me for the role of the youngster in *Hearts of the World*. He won the part, hands down. When I first looked at that four-year-old, I wished he were mine. He was just the sort of boy any man would be proud to call son. It wasn't until now that I felt the deep void of childlessness, but it was there and it wouldn't go away. Each chance I had to gain Ben's affection, such as magic tricks or games, I spent fathering him, and he in turn seemed to understand and return my devotion. When the scene in which he played was done and I was free, we would hurry over to Mrs. Lee's for a dish of ice cream and new tricks at the table. The one he enjoyed most was the handkerchief-match trick. I told him of the gold I had buried in my back yard, and he wanted to go at once and dig it up, but I had already retrieved it by then.

In the lobby of Clune's theater, Los Angeles, I had just witnessed the première showing of *Hearts of the World*. Leaving Nora in her loge seat, I moved about until I was within hearing distance of some rival cameramen. I was pleased to hear the flattering things said about the photography, especially the remarks about the goring pleats in the hat Lillian Gish wore. It contained new photographic qualities I had worked hours to achieve. It needed just the right light on special material to capture the three-dimensional look. I seldom enjoyed seeing a movie, because it had to be dissected and analyzed for flaws. I saw it from a camera angle only. When I was standing under the theater marquee afterward, waiting for my car, Charlie Chaplin sidled up to me with his toothy smile. "How'd you do it, Billy?" he grinned. I was highly flattered by these few words.

Lillian and Griffith remained in the theater, being interviewed by reporters. After their sojourn in foreign lands together, it was only natural for the press to hope for an announcement of a personal nature. They didn't get it, so they tried to invent it. Joe Atkinson, from one of the Hollywood trade papers, tried to put words in my mouth.

"What's between Griffith and Gish?" he asked.

"Nothing. How could there be? She is always chaperoned by her mother or Kate Bruce, and besides, when would they have time?"

"Billy, let me tell you some of the facts of life. Don't be such a dumb ass. There's always the lunch hour, you know."

"Is that a fact?" I jammed the stogie into my mouth to show my displeasure. Reporters buzz at you like a mosquito until they get blood. This time he got no help from me.

It was against such scandalous rumors that Griffith built a private dining room for himself, in the style of the Cheshire Cheese in England. He employed an excellent chef and a waiter to serve his meals. Griffith could now have his meals in private, or with invited guests. It spared him the intrusions a director was often subjected to at mealtime. Privacy was denied him when he entered a public place. Now he had guaranteed privacy.

Mr. Griffith was less concerned about money than anyone I ever knew. When I first worked with him, his forgetting to pick up change in restaurants, I imagined, was due to his deep involvement with his work. Through the years when we worked side by side, the few times he would mention money was when he needed it and found none in his trouser pocket. He never carried a billfold, just used to double bills up in his fist and cram them into his trousers like a handful of lettuce. If he were buttonholed with a sob story, which he might sense wasn't entirely true, he would fish in his pocket, separate a bill, and, without looking at its denomination, hand it to the person. He never became annoyed or angry.

One interesting point about *Hearts of the World*, when we completed it in Hollywood, is that there were five Harrons in it. Bobby had the male lead, of course; his mother played a French woman; his two sisters, Jessie and Mary, played her daughters; and his young brother, Johnny, played "a boy with a barrel." Johnny Harron was a likable youngster. When his future as an actor seemed assured, he was killed in an auto accident in Los Angeles. Mrs. Gish, the mother of Lillian and Dorothy, also had a bit in the film as a refugee mother. Except for one or two later appearances with Lillian, Bobby Harron played his last big part as the hero of *Hearts of the World*. He had hoped to star in *Broken Blossoms* and *Way Down East*, as Lillian again did, but Griffith's eyes had spotted a new image, Richard Barthelmess. Griffith tried to make it up by starring Bobby with Lillian in *The Greatest Question*, released after *Broken Blossoms*, but it was too late.

We were between pictures. We had finished *Hearts* and had not become deeply involved with *Broken Blossoms*. Griffith and Mary Pickford now saw each other more often. Doug Fairbanks had been working on our lot, and they had all been interested in the Liberty Bond drive. It was Mary who first brought Thomas Burke's book, *Limehouse Nights*, which contained "The Chink and the Child," to Griffith's attention. He referred it to me, the sounding board. It was during some retakes on the production stage, so I took the book from Mary and promised to peruse it and give an opinion.

As I read the sad little tale about the illegitimate waif, I could envision Battling Burrows, the brute father and welterweight of Shadwell, and the pathetic frail Lucy he used as whipping-post, because she was his and he had a right to do as he pleased with his own, to quote his words. Little Lucy survived his beatings and neglect until she was twelve. The one person in Limehouse to notice her beauty was the poetic young Chinese, Cheng Huan, who showered his love on her until she was killed by Battling Burrows. Cheng avenged her death and ended his own life. I heartily recommended it, and we soon were casting.

Such a delicate subject would be best if not too starkly depicted. I knew this would be the vehicle to combine the three-dimensional camerawork I had used on Lillian's hat pleating with the new soft-focus Sartov had brought with him. While we were busy making tests of Lillian Gish and Dick Barthelmess, Griffith was busy with Mary and Doug, working on a plan for the relief of unemployed movie personnel. It all began with a small intimate group of financially secure friends willing to set up a fund for motion pictures' less fortunate. I believe Mary thought of it first, for she was a very charitable person. She, in turn, passed the idea along to Doug, who got Charlie Chaplin interested. The little group held meetings off the mezzanine floor of the Alexandria Hotel, before word got out. Not being as wealthy as the four members, I was asked to give one hundred a month out of pay, which I gladly donated. This was the formation of the Motion Picture Relief Fund.

Then we began rehearsing the story. One could visualize how gauze shading might be effective. Viewed through the camera, before taking, I would see if one or more thicknesses of gauze should be put over the front of the lens hood. A shield ring went in front of the gauze to keep the reflected light from hitting the gauze surface. When we were perfectly sure all was in order, the next procedure was to burn a hole through part of the gauze through which the main action would be seen. From then on, the gauze required pruning. This burning off would continue until at times very little of the gauze remained and you would have to start all over again.

At this juncture, Griffith bought land in the San Fernando Valley. In the hope of striking oil, he spent a fortune for oil drills and engineers. The soil produced nothing. It was his most expensive hobby, besides women, and it cost him plenty. Only with the rise in property values did he ever get a good return. But he never lost his enthusiasm for property, even after we left California.

I had noticed that lately he spent a good part of his time talking to Sartov and examining the tests made of Carol Dempster. Once he asked me what I thought of her . . . he was considering signing her to a contract.

"She's a very pretty girl," I agreed. "The new type. Full of pep and built for speed. But can she act?"

"That remains to be seen. I'll use her in small parts and see if the public likes her; then I'll go ahead and build her up. She's a trained dancer, swimmer, and all-round good athlete. As you say, she's built for speed."

Although he was only three years younger than I, his tailored clothes and upright athletic bearing made him look ten years younger, young enough to catch the eye of a pretty girl like Carol. Once I saw her in the back lot, with long dark-auburn curls, talking to Griffith. She had called him David! No one ever called him by his first name, and he had responded. I chuckled to myself. I looked around to see if anyone else had witnessed this. Lillian was standing as though transfixed, not far from where I stood. She merely smiled as she passed, and in her usual soft voice said, "There he goes again." She continued walking, with her shoulders straight and her back stiff, that Mona Lisa smile masking her thoughts.

Griffith also ordered tests of Clarine Seymour, another new-type character of the "flaming youth" era that preceded Clara Bow. He called her "Cutie Beautiful"—after her first role, in *The Girl Who Stayed at Home*. She was photogenic, better looking on screen than off. As usual, Clarine was used as a buffer against the other girls, a threat to their standing. In *The Idol Dancer*, Clarine was given better exposure in the title role, as White Almond Flower, with Barthelmess as the beachcomber. The picture was Griffith's second for United Artists, *Broken Blossoms* being the first. Chaplin, Pickford, Fairbanks, and Griffith had united under this banner. Clarine Seymour, the little girl with cold hands, saucer black eyes, and effervescent spirit, was a hard rival for the inexperienced Carol Dempster, although the latter performed very well in the third UA picture, *The Love Flower*—in fact, well enough to make the trade aware she was being groomed for the future.

It occurs to me that perhaps a brief outline, somewhat personal, of D. W. Griffith as I knew him in my sixteen years of association might bring out some facets of his real personality, instead of the glorified descriptions handed out by press agents. Nothing I have read even does justice to his personal traits of character.

Generosity. Giving was one of his deepest virtues. Not only would he give the applicant the first bill he extracted from his pocket, but if the case was more than trivial, he would detail one of his assistants to follow up and help someone in trouble. It was not show-off stuff or ego.

Tolerance. His kindly efforts to produce results were incredible. He might chide the one making a mistake in a gentle manner. "What were you thinking of?" he would ask. "You knew we had to have that article here." Then a full stop, a pause long enough for the error to sink in, which would hurt more than if he had flown into a rage.

Temper. Perhaps at most only a half-dozen times did I ever see him in a rage, and like most extremists, he was over it at once.

Peacemaker. To prevent outbursts, he would act very quickly. If outsiders on location tried to cause a disturbance, he would walk up and ask them to desist, and if that didn't stop them, he would reach in his pocket and pay them to get out. I saw many instances where this was abused, and I stubbornly suggested I wouldn't have paid, only to hear his logical reasoning: "The delay would cost us much more than I paid."

Persistence. Once he had made up his mind to get results, whether of portrayal in acting or some photographic effect, he would keep at it from all angles until successful.

Patience. Even when handling big situations, such as mob scenes, with things going awry, he would break out in snatches of song, a bit of psychology that seemed to calm the excited performers, causing them to be less tense. His bag of tricks was enormous, and if one trick did not work, he would try another. If you did not possess the ability he was searching for, you weren't fired, just demoted. He did it by easy stages, until you realized for yourself you didn't fit and just let yourself out.

Although he called his players children, he was a stern parent if crossed. He would allow the one in error to talk to a finish, during which time he would not say a word. Then, "Well, you know better, of course," after which he would remain silent as a sphinx, leaving you guessing whether you had really won the debate or not.

The tests had all been made for my experimental method of photography for *Broken Blossoms*. This was to be an inexpensive project. The sets were simple and there would be few actors, so the actual shooting time would be fast. In fact, we made the entire picture in eighteen days.

For the first day's shooting, I had placed the lights for the actual taking, but we hadn't gone ahead because so much time had been spent on rehearsing. Lillian Gish was exhausted when the time came for the usual shooting, and Griffith decided to make the shots early next morning after Lillian had rested.

My assistant, Karl Brown, was waiting for me at my gate next day. "Gee, everyone's waiting for you on the set. Mr. Griffith is there, too, and he won't go ahead without you," Karl Brown said. We got there and I rushed in, shedding my coat. The camera, film, and everything were in position, Karl had seen to that; all I had to do was focus. I didn't even take time out to say good morning, but looked hurriedly through the ground glass at Lillian, seated in position, dressed in the finery Cheng Huan (Dick Barthelmess) had decked her out in. I could see just a beautiful face, I hadn't noticed the hair or anything else about her, except her eyes, and on them I focused, making sure only one light reflected in the pupil of her eyes. I closed the camera.

"Lights!" I called to the gaffer. "All ready, Mr. Griffith."

"Camera!" he gave the command for action.

I had ground out but a few feet when Karl, who looked at the lens marks, said nervously, "You forgot to stop your lens!"

"Shut up!" I cautioned. "We'll take it over again anyway."

"But, Mr. Bitzer," Karl insisted, pulling at my sleeve. "You started before all the lights were on. All those top lights you figured out so carefully yesterday were not lit, and some others."

Then I saw I would have to pay more attention or someone, like Sartov, would make me look bad. Anyway, the scene stayed in as it was, and Mr. Griffith did not take it over. He just said at the finish, "Come on, let's move along."

Now the lens I was using was a 3-inch Dallmeyr F.I.9 with a large aperture. It was a lens I never would have used wide open, because of its depth and general fuzziness and uncertainty. This was the fast lens, however, and with the low-key lighting from directions I would not use ordinarily, and my focus on the eyes as I saw them—all this combined with that element of luck made the first beautiful soft-focus head on the screen.

As we developed tests of every scene taken, favorable reports came back. We had a beautiful new atmospheric effect never before seen on film, something that would lend itself to the dull gold sheen I had desired. Throughout the rest of *Broken Blossoms*, I went right on duplicating the lighting and photography.

Lillian's acting was quiet and unemotional. She was an excellent pantomimist, who used her body to express emotion. In *Blossoms* she made her sad, fearful smile by using her fingers to turn up the corners of her mouth when commanded by the sadistic Battling Burrows, her father (Donald Crisp), to smile. For her "trapped animal" scene, when she is cornered in the closet, terrified that Battling Burrows will kill her, Griffith closed off the set so just we three, Griffith, Lillian, and the camera, were present. "Load the camera with plenty of film,

Billy," Griffith said. "I'm going to shoot this scene without stopping, even if it takes all day to do it." Then turning to Lillian, he said, "Are you ready?"

"Yes, Mr. Griffith" was her obedient reply, as she walked into the three-frame closet set.

In a frenzy, Lillian's eyes fair popped out of her head. I began to grind the film, for I could sense that this was it. She began to shake, and the muscles of her face quivered in abject fright. I almost wept at seeing her suffering, while Griffith leaned forward in his director's chair, relishing every moment of it.

I kept cranking the film through the camera until the entire thousand feet were finished and there was no more film. As Lillian came from the closet, Griffith rushed to her and caught her before she slipped into a faint. "Get her maid, Billy, and that will be all for today."

Then to Lillian he spoke words of comfort: "You were just great, Lucy, you were great." The greatest compliment was calling her Lucy, the character's name. I left them alone as I went for her maid.

Griffith thought only in terms of picture-making. His instincts and knowledge worked together. His eyes saw everything, noted everything, with the skill of an artist. He seemed to feel no emotion, no pain, no pity. To be other than dispassionate in this artificial setting would have ruined the performance. All that interested the professional in him was that the performance should have shock value and still seem natural.

The finished picture was a tribute to his dedicated skill, and many writers consider it his best. *Broken Blossoms* was a departure from the tried-and-true formulas. As such it was shocking and needed the soft tones of gold on the prints and the soft focus Sartov created. When shown at the George M. Cohan theater in New York, it was surrounded on the stage frame by Chinese-blue lantern light, giving it soft Oriental tones. While containing none of the spectacular qualities of *The Birth*, it gave us an insight into Lillian's dramatic artistry not seen before and established her as a great dramatic discovery.

When it opened in May 1919, *Broken Blossoms* received rave notices. It made more money in proportion to cost than any picture Griffith ever made, except *The Birth of a Nation*.

Lillian Gish at the waterfront, *Broken Blossoms*

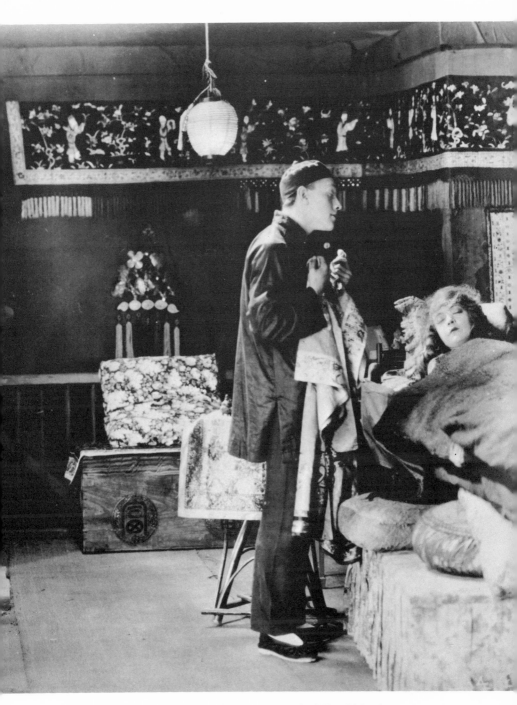

Richard Barthelmess as Cheng Huan, left; with Miss Gish, above

Two shots of the beating and death of Miss Gish. Donald Crisp is her sadistic father, the prizefighter "Battling Burrows"

THIRTEEN

Mamaroneck:
The New Master

Griffith now decided to move back to New York and was in search of new quarters for his company. The Flagler estate on Orienta Point, off the mainland of Mamaroneck, New York, and facing Long Island Sound, was up for sale. Griffith's brother, Albert Grey, Mr. Griffith, the agent, and I drove there in Griffith's Rolls-Royce to look at the property. The agent was in the front seat with Haya, Griffith's Japanese chauffeur.

"I suppose you are familiar with the Flagler legend," the agent said as we rode. "Henry Flagler was one of the richest men in the country, a multimillionaire. He lived like a veritable king, spending money on whims, women, and horses. He married and divorced several times. He knew his money could buy him anything. He owned a railroad, among other things, and practically the entire state of Florida. He used his power there and had a new law passed that enabled him to divorce a wife—she was declared insane, when all other means failed. After that, he isolated himself on his beautiful Orienta Point property, where only those he favored were permitted to join him. You will soon see the place. The regular guard at the entrance is stationed in a tower with a telephone and searchlight."

We had turned into a road and soon came on the tower. Everything was as he had said. The guard came over to the car, recognized the agent, and nodded for him to proceed. We passed over a narrow road which had been built up in the water for the sole purpose of passage to what looked like a small island. There were plenty of giant trees. We stopped again as we came to the first stone house and another gate.

"This," said our guide, "is the caretaker's house."

The caretaker had a gun in his holster in plain sight. He opened the gate and let us pass through to the stately mansion amid the trees. Our car pulled up to the front entrance, and we got out. There were stairs to climb to reach the porch that complemented the heavy mahogany doorway. Through these majestic portals we were ushered into a reception hall. There was a massive stairway, heavily carpeted, wide, and circling at the top. We were led into a banquet hall of gigantic proportion. The walls were covered in rich leather and gold-leaf cloth.

Next we came to the rear of the mansion, where a sunroom extended the full length of the main house. Then we went out on the long porch, which gave a view of the small boats peppering the Sound. Near the end of the point there was also a lovely dollhouse pavilion. At the right of the mansion were a large kitchen and dining room. Under the house was an expansive basement. Facing the kitchen, but separated from the main house, was the servants' seven-room house, a lovely place by itself, with a stone foundation. Flagler had died, and now the estate was up for sale. Griffith had always wished for just such a stately mansion, away from prying eyes, and his eagerness to make this his own movie lot as well as his private domain was apparent. A few days later, the deal was closed and Griffith took over the Flagler estate.

He made the banquet hall his office, furnishing it with a large desk, a couch, a few leather hardback chairs, and cabinets lining the walls. He made a waiting room out of the sunroom, but kept the porch door locked against use. The second-floor master quarters became the wardrobe department, and dressing rooms with lights, stools, chairs, mirrors, and so on. Here, too, were our designers and musicians, filling up all available space. The kitchen and dining room were torn out and used as an indoor stage. The servants' quarters, where Haya and his wife, Haru, lived upstairs, also became a cafeteria below, entered through the shedlike tunnel from the stage exit.

The camera department took over the entire basement. An outside stage was erected, causing the felling of two old majestic oak trees. It was sad to see them go. A film laboratory was now erected, and we were running out of land to build more. The lumber taken from the shucking of the mansion was hauled away by some of the crew. One man, who shall go unnamed, built himself a house from the lumber he purloined.

With Griffith's usual dislike for cold weather, he took the company to Fort Lauderdale, Florida, in December 1919, ostensibly for outdoor shots of two pictures—*The Idol Dancer*, with Clarine Seymour, and *The Love Flower*, with Carol

Dempster. Richard Barthelmess played the male lead in both pictures. Griffith was sold on the versatile Barthelmess and his suave looks. Dick's mother was a former actress, and she held her son very close during his formative period, as do most theatrical mothers. Also, Dick had the advantage of a superior education. His mother was ever by his side, until Mary Hay came into his life and severed the cord, later, during the filming of *Way Down East*.

Not being satisfied with the Fort Lauderdale scenery, Griffith sent two men from our New York office scouting for more tropical country. Jack Lloyd was sent to Cuba and Jack Manning to Nassau, Bahama Islands. Manning made the trip to Nassau, leaving one day and returning the next, with loud cries of "Eureka!" Lloyd found little to recommend Cuba for our settings.

Now in the regular run to Nassau there was an American boat, *The Berry Island*, which was being held up for repairs. The storm season had done much damage not only to the boat but to the coastline as well. Days passed with no transportation in sight, until one day Manning met a young man, named Mank, who had just made the trip over with a load of liquor and now wanted money to buy a boat for rumrunning purposes. He suggested that Manning come see the boat he had in mind. He would buy it, if Griffith would make the trip over with him. There would be no liquor at all upon the boat during the trip over. Griffith looked over the trim little craft, and the price was agreed upon.

The boat was called the *Grey Duck*, about one hundred feet long, nineteen feet wide, beautifully painted white, mahogany trimmed, all brass shining. It should have had only fifteen or twenty passengers at most aboard. Instead we had thirty-seven. Dick Barthelmess, his mother, and Kate Bruce were not with us, for Dick could not be separated from his mother, who wanted a more comfortable trip. Mank did not sail with us, but the previous owner did. Mank had another boat which was to follow us in a day or two, so he switched his regular pilot over to the second boat and used his assistant, a native boy, on the *Grey Duck*.

We put out of the harbor, waving happily to those who would follow. It was a day filled with tropical loveliness. Our food supply consisted of large bushel baskets of Florida's most delectable fruits, many beautifully prepared sandwiches, and a goodly supply of canned goods. We had ample water for the day, but no ice or liquor refreshments. Just the necessities of life for a one-day outing.

I, being at heart a commoner, decided to look in upon the crew and make contact at first hand. I found half the crew in the engine room—one young Bahamian. The first thing I learned about the *Grey Duck* was that we were in the hands of an amateur. With this fact established, I found the rest of the crew, a youngish, rather skinny, and weak-looking seaman. "You must be a sailor of vast experience to work this ship alone. Tell me, have you been following the sea long?"

"I should say not!" he replied indignantly. "I've only been going to sea about three months. I came down here, went broke on the horses, and the only job around was deckhand on this rumrunner. So here I am."

I went aft without receiving any more bad news. A practically unmanned ship. A green crew of one engineer who could only operate when the engine was performing right and one deckhand who had never piloted before.

When I reached the aft end of the vessel, my fears somewhat evaporated at the sight of my happy companions. Carefree and laughing, at peace with the world. It was only a short trip anyway. By the rail on the fantail deck sat Griffith. Over by the rail, her fine eyes sparkling with life and pleasure, stood Carol Dempster. She was much amused by the antics of Porter Strong and his parrot. Day was passing, and everything was as it should be. We had eaten our fill of the fruit and sandwiches. Soon we would be in Nassau, where we could again stretch out and rest after a delightful day.

Then I went up on deck and learned we were slightly off course. Nightfall was coming on and we were not yet sighting Nassau. We passed a small group of islands, then continued on. The boat was pitching about on its uncertain course. Griffith moved closer to Carol at the rail. They were looking into the darkness. Carol motioned to the islands we had just passed; then Griffith nodded and gave orders to have the boat return there until morning. We dropped anchor in a protected cove. The weather was kindly and mild, but even so, sleeping was difficult in such cramped quarters.

In the morning, we could perceive a storm was going on in the sea-lane we must travel if we wished to reach Nassau. We stayed put. Our food supply was running low, so my nephew Lou and several of the boys rigged up fishing poles, and Lou caught the first fish. It was a real beauty and he was proud of his fisherman's skill. He even cooked it and it tasted good. The fish which had been driven in by the storm, however, were not fit to eat. Jack Lloyd became so ill that he turned a greenish hue. We needed a doctor and there was none aboard.

"If I could get him over to the island, there might be someone there who could help him," Manning volunteered. He rowed one of our lifeboats to the island, where he was met by a native who helped him get Jack to a hut wherein an old woman lived. I doubt if he could have fallen into better hands; she mixed a brew which Jack had to drink and stuck a feather down his throat, which set him to vomit the poison out. The cure was so good that Jack was once more able to carry his own weight. Instead of returning to the boat, they set out to look for food.

They had been gone so long that even Griffith was worried, especially about Lloyd. He got a boat and rowed over to find what was detaining them. When he found them, Griffith was amazed at Lloyd's recovery and Manning's hilarity, until a whiff of Manning's breath gave him a clue.

"Hey," he grinned, "where'd you get the monkey milk?"

They led Griffith back to the house of plenty and fed him a piece of corn bread and a drink of the monkey milk. Thoroughly enjoying himself, Griffith had them bake a large cake for those on the boat. The Southerner in Griffith seemed to understand these people, for he also persuaded them to kill their five chickens and cook them. Of course he paid heavily for this, as always. Five chickens wasn't much for thirty-seven people, but it was good food. Then there was the corn bread and what canned food we had left, and on the morrow we would surely be under way.

But the next day the storm persisted and we had to stay in our cove to keep out of it. We made numerous trips to the island for water. We felt cross and itchy. Sanitation was a thing of the past by now. On the fourth day it was a case of do or die. We just couldn't stay there forever; storm or no storm, we had to go.

We set off once more. First there was heavy rain that dropped in torrential violence. Then suddenly the little boat gave a jerk, just for a second. Then it seemed to pause another second, as though getting its bearings. When it happened I was down in the cabin, staying out of the rain. Now I went up on deck to look at the sky. Off to the northeast loomed a cloud bank, a frowning gray mass, and on the horizon it was black. The wind was blowing strong in my face and I could barely see. The prow of the little ship rose and fell, when suddenly I heard Griffith sing out, "Blow ye winds, blow. Let her rock."

I had a feeling the boss had blown his stack, but others were enjoying the tempest, so I went to hide my misgivings. But the next time the boat rolled, there was no pause or still-ness; instead she made a funny sort of dip and I heard the mighty splash of waves against her tiny planks. It seemed to me to be getting rougher and tougher. Now the boat was pitching and rolling. I went back up, climbing the stairs in a drunken manner. Sure enough, the waves were foaming up and breaking into whitecaps. In just half an hour the wind had risen to such velocity the waves no longer slapped at the side of the ship, they pounded with sudden booming strokes, mak-ing the planks tremble. An abashed Griffith was looking to-ward the pilothouse. Suddenly the air was rent by an unearthly scream.

I rushed below. There in a corner were Bert Sutch and his wife on their knees, praying with a group. In a corner stood Porter Strong, a razor in hand, mad with fright, panic-stricken and ready to cut the throat of his mascot parrot. This was real, no one was acting. Griffith and Carol came rushing down directly behind me.

"Calm yourselves, children," Griffith intoned in a cool, con-trolled voice I am sure he was far from feeling. "We'll be out of this in a few minutes. I'll order the ship back to the haven we just left."

Our ship returned to the cove before much damage had

been done. We were out of the tempest and back to sunshine and tranquillity. There was also good news waiting for us. The regular pilot of the *Grey Duck* was nearby in another cove. He, too, had been driven back by the storm. Word was sent to him of our dire need of his steady hand to bring us safely into Nassau. He knew the boat and the waters, and when it was established he would take charge, all fears disappeared. Strange to say, there were no more storms to threaten our safe landing.

Sunday morning found us in Nassau. The church bells were ringing, as they always did when a ship was sighted, but this time it was different. Many anxious moments had been caused when the *Grey Duck* was reported by the press to be lost at sea. Our New York office had sent out planes to find us, but they had been unsuccessful, due to the storms and our nesting in the reef in a small boat. Coast Guard boats had also been unable to find us and were driven back to Miami. The New York newspapers issued hourly reports and extras which kept the public on edge for days. It could all have ended in tragedy. Everyone on that boat was able to read his own obit upon his return, for all hope had been abandoned for the ship and all of us on it. Naturally, when we turned up, it was claimed that we had staged the whole thing as a publicity stunt for our pictures. We never admitted that it was just plain stupidity.

One of my fondest memories is of the Bahama Islands and the beautiful people who live there. The filming of outdoor footage for *The Idol Dancer* and *The Love Flower* was over all too soon; then we flew back to New York for studio work at Mamaroneck. Soon we would be on our way to New England for part of the footage of *Way Down East*. The rest of it we photographed at the new studio in Mamaroneck. We had safely reached the summit, set by Griffith, and the applause had been mighty. It was now time to relax and rest on our laurels.

On location at White River Junction, Vermont, for *Way Down East*, 1920. The sleigh took Lillian Gish and Billy Bitzer to the river site

Shooting the barn-dance scene of *Way Down East* at Mamaroneck. Bitzer is in soft hat behind camera; Griffith is sitting in front of camera

Griffith hamming it up on location for *Way Down East*. Bitzer behind him with camera, Henrik Sartov in cap and glasses at his left

A Bitzer still of Griffith directing the famous "never darken these doors again" scene in *Way Down East*

Griffith's return from being "lost at sea" on the *Grey Duck*, right.
Kate Bruce, center, and Richard Barthelmess, left

On location in Louisiana for *The White Rose*, 1923. The pregnant
Mae Marsh is about to attempt suicide. Griffith in front of camera at
right, Bitzer behind it

On location in Florida for *The White Rose*. Ivor Novello and Mae Marsh are the actors. Bitzer and Sartov are behind Griffith's chair

--⊰ FOURTEEN ⊱--

The End of an Era

Ahead lay heartbreak days. New types of cameras and cameramen were appearing everywhere. Our movie actors were being replaced by persons who had learned their techniques on
Broadway. The lot in Mamaroneck was humming with new
types of movie people—designers, sound technicians, financial
men, efficiency men, businessmen. Neither Griffith nor I could
be his own man. We were heavily in debt. We belonged to
the corporation, the very thing we had fought at Biograph and
the reason Griffith had left there. I had been slow to follow
him, but he had convinced me we must leave if we were going
to amount to anything. Now the business office was completely on top again.

After we made *Way Down East*, my part in the making of
Griffith films was that of just another cameraman, though my
name still had some screen value. The Pathé camera, which I
had worked with throughout so much of my career, was

scorned by all but me. Stubbornly I clung to it, and was re-
viled and ridiculed. I took to staying away from the set as
much as possible. When the studio called, I made excuses for
not reporting.

On opening night of *Way Down East,* we repaired to the
theater for the première as usual. Bobby Harron was missing
that night. He had shot himself accidentally in his rooms at
the Algonquin Hotel. While unpacking his dress suit, he was
fatally wounded by a revolver that he had wrapped in his coat.
A report went out that he had been unhappy over the roles he
was getting, or not getting, and his death was suicide. But I
know better. He lived a couple of days, long enough to make
his confession and receive the sacraments from Father William
Humphrey, who rushed to his bedside when he heard the
news. This was the priest who had brought him as a boy to
the old Biograph studio on Fourteenth Street. Bobby would
not have lied to him as he saw death approach.

His death marked the end of an era. With Bobby's passing,
some thread of unity seemed to leave us. A feeling of guilt lay
heavy on all of us. It was a falling away and breaking up of
our former trust and friendship. We felt that Bobby had
brought us luck when he came to us so young and eager. I
can still see his face as I photographed *Bobby's Kodak* early in
1908, when Lawrence Griffith was merely the name of another
actor. After Bobby's death in 1920, it was never the same
again.

As we left, one by one, Griffith seemed quite alone and isolated. I think it was this isolation more than anything—money
or fame—that gave him trouble, although it may have simply
been the changing times and the beginning of a new era.

On location in Farmington, New York, to film *America*, 1924. Griffith is wearing straw hat

Filming the "Era of Peace" scene of *America* in Summit, New York. Note cannons and war machines covered with vines

The guillotine set for *Orphans of the Storm* at Mamaroneck, New York. Bitzer in white shirt under umbrella at right, Sartov under umbrella at left

Bitzer instructing Babe Ruth in the use of a 16 mm. hand camera

Billy and Ethel Bitzer attending the première of *Lady of the Pavements* in 1929

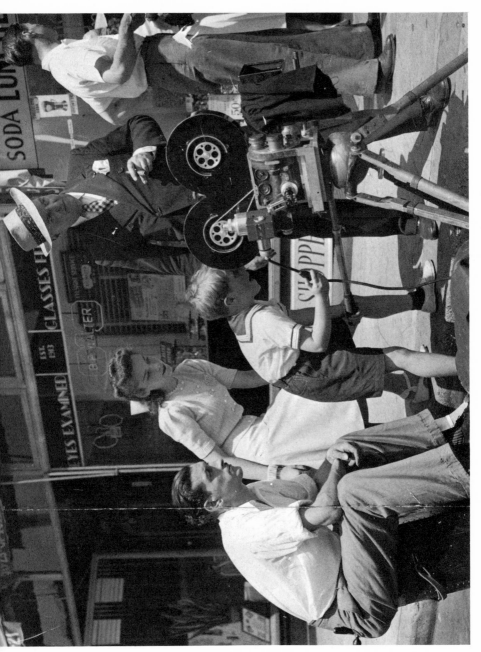

Bitzer in 1940 with his son, Eden Griffith Bitzer, age six, at the camera

Reassembling the old Biograph camera at the Museum of Modern Art, 1940. *Photo by Eliot Elisofon*

Bitzer and a portrait of Griffith at the MOMA. *Photo by Eliot Elisofon*

Note

G. W. Bitzer died in Los Angeles on April 29, 1944. To complete the story from the point at which his manuscript breaks off, his marriage to the second Mrs. Bitzer (née Ethel Boddy) took place on April 5, 1923; their son, Eden Griffith Bitzer, was born on April 7, 1934.

Against the opposition of the Hollywood producers, Billy Bitzer in 1926 founded the International Photographers of the Motion Picture Industries (IPMPI), of which he was twice president, and he was proud of his honorary life membership in local 644 IATSE. After *Way Down East* he worked as one of several cameramen on five Griffith films—*The White Rose*, 1923; *America*, 1924; *Drums of Love*, 1927; *The Battle of the Sexes*, 1928, a remake of the 1914 film; and *Lady of the Pavements*, 1929.

In 1939, before his first heart attack, he was asked by the Museum of Modern Art to collate and annotate old Biograph Bulletins and other materials donated to their archives; while doing this, he began to write down his recollections and record the events that make up the substance of this book. (A page of his original handwritten manuscript is reproduced on page 133; see the printed text on page 132 for comparison.) In the winter of 1943 he was hospitalized, and in January 1944 he was sent to California by his doctor to avoid the New York winter, and went for recuperation to the Motion Picture Country Home at Woodland Hills.

In one of his last letters to his wife, Ethel, dated thirteen days before he died, he characteristically wrote: "D.W., Mary, and Lillian came here the day before I arrived. They thought that I was already here. Pretty swell of them, don't you think?"

THE FILMS OF G. W. BITZER

*Names in parenthesis are those of co-cameramen; listings are
according to release dates*

1896

WILLIAM MC KINLEY AT
   CANTON, OHIO (DICKSON)
HARD WASH

1897

PRESIDENT MC KINLEY'S IN-
   AUGURATION (DICKSON)
MUTOSCOPE SHORTS

1898

U.S.S. MAINE, HAVANA HARBOR
SPANISH-AMERICAN WAR SCENES

1899

JIM JEFFRIES–TOM SHARKEY
   FIGHT (WM. A. BRADY
   PRODUCTION)
AMBULANCE CORPS DRILL

CHILDREN FEEDING DUCKLINGS
HOW DUCKS ARE FATTENED
TRAIN ON JACOB'S LADDER, MT.
   WASHINGTON
FRANKENSTEIN TRESTLE, WHITE
   MTS.
CANADIAN PACIFIC RAILROAD
   SHOTS
UNION PACIFIC RAILROAD SHOTS
THE PICTURESQUE WEST

1900

GALVESTON HURRICANE SHOTS
POLO GAMES, BROOKLYN
THE INTERRUPTED MESSAGE
TOUGH KID'S WATERLOO
GRAND TRUNK RAILROAD SCENES
WATER DUEL
LOVE IN THE SUBURBS

247

LAST ALARM
U.S. NAVAL MILITIA
COUNCIL BLUFFS TO OMAHA—
TRAIN SCENIC
CHILDHOOD'S VOWS
AT BREAKNECK SPEED (FALL
RIVER, MASS.)

1901
MIDDIES SHORTENING SAIL
BOATS UNDER OARS
PAN-AMERICAN EXPOSITION
ELECTRIC TOWER (INCL.
NIGHT SHOTS)
UNION PACIFIC RAILROAD SCENES
IN THE GRAZING COUNTRY
FATTENED FOR THE MARKET

1902
ST. LOUIS EXPOSITION

1903
I WANT MY DINNER
N.Y. CITY FIRE DEPT.
AMERICAN SOLDIER IN LOVE AND
WAR
BOY IN THE BARREL
DUDE AND THE BURGLARS
DONT GET GAY WITH YOUR
MANICURE
MODEL COURTSHIP
JEFFRIES–CORBETT FIGHT
(RESTAGED)
HAPPY HOOLIGAN EARNS HIS
DINNER

HOW MIKE GOT THE SOAP IN
HIS EYES
IN THE N.Y. SUBWAY
KIDNAPPER
PHYSICAL CULTURE GIRLS
POOR OLD FIDO
PRESIDENT T. R. ROOSEVELT,
JULY 4TH
PROFESSOR OF THE DRAMA
PAJAMA GIRL
SWEETS FOR THE SWEET
SHOCKING INCIDENT
SHE FELL FAINTING IN HIS
ARMS
TOO ARDENT LOVER
UNPROTECTED FEMALE
UNFAITHFUL WIFE
WAGES OF SIN
WIDOW
WILLIE'S CAMERA
WHY FOXY GRANDPA ESCAPED
DUCKING
WEIGHING THE BABY
YOU WILL SEND ME TO BED,
EH?

1904
AUTO BOAT ON THE HUDSON
VANDERBILT CUP AUTO RACE
HOLLAND SUBMARINE TORPEDO
BOAT
CHILDREN IN THE SURF
CONEY ISLAND POLICE PATROL
CHICKEN THIEF
FIRST BABY
HERO OF LIAO YANG

JUDGE ALTON B. PARKER
LOST CHILD
MOONSHINERS
PERSONAL
RACING THE CHUTES AT
    DREAMLAND
SEASHORE BABY
SLOCUM DISASTER
SPEED TEST OF TARANTULA
SWIMMING CLASS
TWO BOTTLE BABIES
WIDOW AND THE ONLY MAN

1905

AL TRELEOR MUSCLE EXERCISES
ATHLETIC GIRL AND BURGLAR
AUTO RACES, ORMONDE, FLA.
BALLROOM TRAGEDY
BARNSTORMERS
BETWEEN THE DANCES
CHAUNCEY EXPLAINS
COUNTRY COURTSHIP
DREAM OF THE RACETRACK
    FIEND
DEER STALKING WITH CAMERA
DEPARTURE OF TRAIN FROM
    STATION
DEADWOOD SLEEPER
EVERYBODY WORKS BUT FATHER
FIREBUG
FLIGHT OF LUDLOW'S AERO-
    DROME
FUN ON THE JOY LINE
GEE, IF ME MUDDER COULD
    SEE ME
GOSSIPERS

GREAT JEWEL MYSTERY
    (DOBSON)
HENPECKED HUSBAND
HIS MOVE
HORSE THIEF
IMPOSSIBLE CONVICTS
KENTUCKY FEUD
LEAP FROG RAILWAY
LUDLOW'S AEROPLANE
LIFTING THE LID
MOBILIZING MASS. STATE
    TROOPS
MOOSE HUNT IN CANADA
MYSTERY OF THE JEWEL
    CASKET (DOBSON)
NAN PATERSON'S TRIAL
OSLERIZING PAPA
PIPE DREAM
QUAIL SHOOTING, PINEHURST
REUBEN IN THE SUBWAY
RIVER PIRATES
RECEPTION OF BRITISH FLEET
SALMON FISHING, QUEBEC
SPARRING AT N.Y. ATHLETIC
    CLUB
SIMPLE LIFE
SPIRIT OF '76
TROUT FISHING, RANGELEY
    LAKES
TURKEY HUNT, PINEHURST
TWO TOPERS
UNDER THE BAMBOO TREE
WINE OPENER
WEDDING
WRESTLING, N.Y. ATHLETIC
    CLUB

1906

AT THE MONKEY HOUSE
BLACK HAND
COUNTRY SCHOOLMASTER
CRITIC (DOBSON)
DR. DIPPY'S SANITARIUM
FOX HUNT
FRIEND IN NEED IS FRIEND
   INDEED
GATEWAY TO THE CATSKILLS
GRAND HOTEL TO BIG INDIAN
HALLROOM BOYS
HOLDUP OF ROCKY MT. EXPRESS
IN THE HAUNTS OF RIP VAN
   WINKLE
IN THE HEART OF THE CATSKILLS
LIGHTHOUSE
MARRIED FOR MILLIONS
MASQUERADERS
MR. BUTT-IN
MR. HURRY-UP
NIGHT OF THE PARTY
PAYMASTER
POUGHKEEPSIE REGATTA
SAN FRANCISCO
SOCIETY BALLOONING
SUBPOENA SERVER
TRIAL MARRIAGES
THROUGH AUSTIN GLEN
VALLEY OF ESOPUS
VILLAGE CUT-UP (DOBSON)

1907

CRAYONO
DEAF-MUTES BALL
DR. SKINUM

ELOPEMENT
FALSELY ACCUSED
FENCING MASTER
FIGHTS OF NATIONS
HYPNOTIST'S REVENGE
IF YOU HAD A WIFE LIKE THIS
JAMESTOWN EXPOSITION
LOVE MICROBE
MODEL'S MA
MRS. SMITHERS' BOARDING
   SCHOOL
NEIGHBORS
PROFESSIONAL JEALOUSY
RUBE BROWN IN TOWN
TENDERLOIN TRAGEDY
TERRIBLE TED
TRUANTS
UNDER THE OLD APPLE TREE
WIFE WANTED
YALE LAUNDRY

1908

BOBBY'S KODAK
CLASSMATES
LONESOME JUNCTION
SNOWMAN
BOY DETECTIVE
PRINCESS IN THE VASE
YELLOW PERIL
CAUGHT BY WIRELESS
FAMOUS ESCAPE
HER FIRST ADVENTURE
OLD ISAACS, THE PAWNBROKER
HIS DAY OF REST
HULDA'S LOVERS
KING OF THE CANNIBAL ISLANDS

KING'S MESSENGER

MIXED BABIES

MUSIC MASTER

ROMANCE OF AN EGG

SCULPTOR'S NIGHTMARE

WHEN KNIGHTS WERE BOLD

AT THE FRENCH BALL

INVISIBLE FLUID

MAN IN THE BOX (MARVIN)

NIGHT OF TERROR

'OSTLER JOE

OUTLAW

OVER THE HILLS TO THE POOR-
HOUSE

THOMPSON'S NIGHT OUT

BLACK VIPER (MARVIN)

FIGHT FOR FREEDOM (MARVIN)

KENTUCKIAN (MARVIN)

*CALAMITOUS ELOPEMENT
(MARVIN)

DECEIVED SLUMMING PARTY
(MARVIN)

MAN AND THE WOMAN
(MARVIN)

BETRAYED BY A HANDPRINT
(MARVIN)

MONDAY MORNING IN A CONEY
ISLAND POLICE COURT

SMOKED HUSBAND

STOLEN JEWELS

WHERE BREAKERS ROAR
(MARVIN)

ZULU'S HEART

THE BARBARIAN, INGOMAR

CONCEALING A BURGLAR

DEVIL

FATHER GETS IN THE GAME

MR. JONES AT THE BALL

PLANTER'S WIFE

ROMANCE OF A JEWESS

VAQUERO'S VOW

AFTER MANY YEARS

THE GUERRILLA (MARVIN)

THE INGRATE (MARVIN)

MONEY MAD

PIRATE'S GOLD (MARVIN)

SONG OF THE SHIRT

TAMING OF THE SHREW
(MARVIN)

CHRISTMAS BURGLARS

CLUBMAN AND THE TRAMP

FEUD AND THE TURKEY
(MARVIN)

RECKONING

TEST OF FRIENDSHIP

VALET'S WIFE (MARVIN)

1909

THE CURTAIN POLE

MRS. JONES ENTERTAINS

THE MANIAC COOK

THE CHRISTMAS BURGLARS

A WREATH IN TIME

THE HONOR OF THIEVES

THE CRIMINAL HYPNOTIST

THE SACRIFICE

THE WELCOME BURGLAR

A RURAL ELOPEMENT

MR. JONES HAS A CARD PARTY

THE HINDOO DAGGER

*Bitzer's first film with D. W. Griffith.

THE SALVATION ARMY LASS

LOVE FINDS A .WAY

TRAGIC LOVE

THE GIRLS AND DADDY

THOSE BOYS (MARVIN)

THE CORD OF LIFE (MARVIN)

TRYING TO GET ARRESTED
(MARVIN)

THE FASCINATING MRS. FRANCES

THOSE AWFUL HATS

JONES AND THE LADY BOOK
AGENT

THE DRIVE FOR LIFE (MARVIN)

THE BRAHMA DIAMOND

THE POLITICIAN'S LOVE STORY
(MARVIN)

THE JONES' AMATEUR THEATRI-
CALS

EDGAR ALLEN POE

THE ROUE'S HEART

HIS WARD'S LOVE

AT THE ALTAR (MARVIN)

THE PRUSSIAN SPY

THE MEDICINE BOTTLE

THE DECEPTION

THE LURE OF THE GOWN
(MARVIN)

LADY HELEN'S ESCAPADE

A FOOL'S REVENGE

THE WOODEN LEG (MARVIN)

I DID IT, MAMA

A BURGLAR'S MISTAKE
(MARVIN)

THE VOICE OF THE VIOLIN
(MARVIN)

A LITTLE CHILD SHALL LEAD
THEM

THE FRENCH DUEL (MARVIN)

JONES AND HIS NEW NEIGHBORS

A DRUNKARD'S REFORMATION

THE WINNING COAT

A RUDE HOSTESS

THE EAVESDROPPER (MARVIN)

CONFIDENCE (MARVIN)

LUCKY JIM (MARVIN)

A SOUND SLEEPER (MARVIN)

A TROUBLESOME SATCHEL
(MARVIN)

'TIS AN ILL WIND (MARVIN)

THE SUICIDE CLUB (MARVIN)

RESURRECTION (MARVIN)

ONE BUSY HOUR (MARVIN)

A BABY'S SHOE (MARVIN)

ELOPING WITH AUNTIE
(MARVIN)

THE CRICKET ON THE HEARTH
(MARVIN)

THE JILT (MARVIN)

ERADICATING AUNTIE (MARVIN)

WHAT DRINK DID

HER FIRST BISCUITS

THE VIOLIN MAKER OF
CREMONA

TWO MEMORIES

THE LONELY VILLA

THE PEACH-BASKET HAT
(MARVIN)

THE SON'S RETURN (MARVIN)

HIS DUTY (MARVIN)

A NEW TRICK

THE NECKLACE

THE WAY OF MAN
THE FADED LILLIES
THE MESSAGE
THE FRIEND OF THE FAMILY
WAS JUSTICE SERVED?
MRS. JONES' LOVER
THE MEXICAN SWEETHEART
THE COUNTRY DOCTOR
JEALOUSY AND THE MAN
THE RENUNCIATION
THE CARDINAL'S CONSPIRACY
THE SEVENTH DAY
TENDER HEARTS
A CONVICT'S SACRIFICE
SWEET AND TWENTY
THE SLAVE
THEY WOULD ELOPE (HIGGIN-
  SON)
MRS. JONES' BURGLAR
  (MARVIN)
THE MENDED LUTE
INDIAN RUNNER'S ROMANCE
WITH HER CARD
THE BETTER WAY
HIS WIFE'S VISITOR
THE MILLS OF THE GODS
OH, UNCLE!
THE SEALED ROOM
1776, OR HESSIAN RENEGADES
  (MARVIN)
THE LITTLE DARLING
IN OLD KENTUCKY
THE CHILDREN'S FRIEND
COMATA, THE SIOUX
GETTING EVEN
THE BROKEN LOCKET

A FAIR EXCHANGE
THE AWAKENING
PIPPA PASSES (MARVIN)
LEATHER STOCKING (MARVIN)
FOOLS OF FATE
WANTED, A CHILD
THE LITTLE TEACHER (MARVIN)
A CHANGE OF HEART
HIS LOST LOVE
LINES OF WHITE ON THE SULLEN
  SEA
THE GIBSON GODDESS
IN THE WATCHES OF THE
  NIGHT
THE EXPIATION
WHAT'S YOUR HURRY?
THE RESTORATION
NURSING A VIPER
TWO WOMEN AND A MAN
THE LIGHT THAT CAME
A MIDNIGHT ADVENTURE
  (MARVIN)
THE OPEN GATE
SWEET REVENGE
THE MOUNTAINEER'S HONOR
IN THE WINDOW RECESS
THE TRICK THAT FAILED
THE DEATH DISK
THROUGH THE BREAKERS
IN A HEMPEN BAG
A CORNER IN WHEAT
THE REDMAN'S VIEW
THE TEST (MARVIN)
A TRAP FOR SANTA CLAUS
IN LITTLE ITALY

TO SAVE HER SOUL (MARVIN)
CHOOSING A HUSBAND

1910
THE ROCKY ROAD (MARVIN)
THE DANCING GIRL OF BUTTE
HER TERRIBLE ORDEAL
THE CALL
THE HONOR OF HIS FAMILY
  (MARVIN)
ON THE REEF
THE LAST DEAL
ONE NIGHT AND THEN
THE CLOISTER'S TOUCH
  (MARVIN)
THE WOMAN FROM MELLON'S
THE DUKE'S PLAN
THE ENGLISHMAN AND THE
  GIRL
THE FINAL SETTLEMENT
  (MARVIN)
HIS LAST BURGLARY
TAMING A HUSBAND
THE NEWLYWEDS (MARVIN)
THE THREAD OF DESTINY
IN OLD CALIFORNIA
THE MAN
THE CONVERTS
FAITHFUL (MARVIN)
THE TWISTED TRAIL
GOLD IS NOT ALL
AS IT IS IN LIFE
A RICH REVENGE
ROMANCE OF THE WESTERN
  HILLS
THOU SHALT NOT

THE WAY OF THE WORLD
THE UNCHANGING SEA
THE GOLD SEEKERS (MARVIN)
LOVE AMONG THE ROSES
  (MARVIN)
THE TWO BROTHERS (MARVIN)
UNEXPECTED HELP
RAMONA
OVER SILENT PATHS
THE IMPALEMENT (MARVIN)
IN THE SEASON OF BUDS
  (MARVIN)
A CHILD OF THE GHETTO
  (MARVIN)
IN THE BORDER STATES
A VICTIM OF JEALOUSY
THE FACE AT THE WINDOW
THE MARKED TIMETABLE
A CHILD'S IMPULSE (MARVIN)
MUGGSY'S FIRST SWEETHEART
THE PURGATION
A MIDNIGHT CUPID
WHAT THE DAISY SAID
A CHILD'S FAITH
THE CALL TO ARMS
SERIOUS SIXTEEN (MARVIN)
A FLASH OF LIGHT
AS THE BELLS RANG OUT
THE ARCADIAN MAID
HOUSE WITH THE CLOSED
  SHUTTERS
HER FATHER'S PRIDE
A SALUTARY LESSON
THE USURER
SORROWS OF THE UNFAITHFUL
IN LIFE'S CYCLE

WILFUL PEGGY

A SUMMER IDYLL

THE MODERN PRODIGAL

ROSE O' SALEM TOWN

LITTLE ANGELS OF LUCK

A MOHAWK'S WAY

THE OATH AND THE MAN

THE ICONOCLAST

EXAMINATION DAY AT SCHOOL

THAT CHINK AT GOLDEN GULCH

THE BROKEN DOLL

THE BANKER'S DAUGHTERS

THE MESSAGE OF THE VIOLIN

TWO LITTLE WAIFS

WAITER NO. 5

THE FUGITIVE

SIMPLE CHARITY (MARVIN)

SONG OF THE WILDWOOD FLUTE

A CHILD'S STRATAGEM

SUNSHINE SUE

A PLAIN SONG

HIS SISTER-IN-LAW

THE GOLDEN SUPPER

THE LESSON

1911

WHEN A MAN LOVES

WINNING BACK HIS LOVE

HIS TRUST

HIS TRUST FULFILLED

A WREATH OF ORANGE BLOSSOMS

THE ITALIAN BARBER

THE TWO PATHS

CONSCIENCE

THREE SISTERS

A DECREE OF DESTINY

FATE'S TURNING

WHAT SHALL WE DO WITH OUR OLD?

THE DIAMOND STAR

THE LILY OF THE TENEMENTS

HEART BEATS OF LONG AGO

FISHER FOLKS

HIS DAUGHTER

THE LONEDALE OPERATOR

WAS HE A COWARD?

TEACHING DAD TO LIKE HER

THE SPANISH GYPSY

THE BROKEN CROSS

THE CHIEF'S DAUGHTER

A KNIGHT OF THE ROAD

MADAME REX

HIS MOTHER'S SCARF

HOW SHE TRIUMPHED

IN THE DAYS OF '49

THE TWO SIDES

THE NEW DRESS

ENOCH ARDEN (PART ONE)

ENOCH ARDEN (PART TWO)

THE WHITE ROSE OF THE WILDS

THE CROOKED ROAD

A ROMANY TRAGEDY

A SMILE OF A CHILD

THE PRIMAL CALL

THE JEALOUS HUSBAND

THE INDIAN BROTHERS

THE THIEF AND THE GIRL

HER SACRIFICE

BLIND PRINCESS AND THE POET

FIGHTING BLOOD

THE LAST DROP OF WATER

BOBBY THE COWARD

A COUNTRY CUPID
THE RULING PASSION
THE ROSE OF KENTUCKY
THE SORROWFUL EXAMPLE
SWORDS AND HEARTS
THE STUFF HEROES ARE MADE
    OF
OLD CONFECTIONER'S MISTAKE
THE UNVEILING
THE ETERNAL MOTHER
DAN THE DANDY
REVENUE MAN AND THE GIRL
THE SQUAW'S LOVE (HIGGINSON,
    MAHR)
ITALIAN BLOOD
THE MAKING OF A MAN
HER AWAKENING
THE ADVENTURES OF BILLY
THE LONG ROAD
THE BATTLE
LOVE IN THE HILLS
THE TRAIL OF THE BOOKS
THROUGH DARKENED VALES
SAVED FROM HIMSELF
A WOMAN SCORNED
THE MISER'S HEART
THE FAILURE
SUNSHINE THROUGH THE DARK
AS IN A LOOKING-GLASS
A TERRIBLE DISCOVERY
THE VOICE OF THE CHILD

1912

A TALE OF THE WILDERNESS
THE BABY AND THE STORK
THE OLD BOOKKEEPER

A SISTER'S LOVE
FOR HIS SON
THE TRANSFORMATION OF MIKE
A BLOT ON THE 'SCUTCHEON
BILLY'S STRATAGEM
THE SUNBEAM
A STRING OF PEARLS
THE ROOT OF EVIL
THE MENDER OF THE NETS
UNDER BURNING SKIES
A SIREN OF IMPULSE
IOLA'S PROMISE
THE GODDESS OF SAGEBRUSH
    GULCH
THE GIRL AND HER TRUST
THE PUNISHMENT
FATE'S INTERCEPTION
THE FEMALE OF THE SPECIES
JUST LIKE A WOMAN
ONE IS BUSINESS, THE OTHER
    CRIME
THE LESSER EVIL
THE OLD ACTOR
A LODGING FOR THE NIGHT
HIS LESSON
WHEN KINGS WERE THE LAW
A BEAST AT BAY
AN OUTCAST AMONG OUTCASTS
HOME FOLKS
A TEMPORARY TRUCE
THE SPIRIT AWAKENED
LENA AND THE GEESE
AN INDIAN SUMMER
THE SCHOOLTEACHER AND THE
    WAIF
MAN'S LUST FOR GOLD

MAN'S GENESIS

HEAVEN AVENGES

A PUEBLO LEGEND

THE SANDS OF DEE

BLACK SHEEP

THE NARROW ROAD

A CHILD'S REMORSE

THE INNER CIRCLE

A CHANGE OF SPIRIT

AN UNSEEN ENEMY

TWO DAUGHTERS OF EVE

FRIENDS

SO NEAR, YET SO FAR

A FEUD IN THE KENTUCKY
  HILLS

IN THE AISLES OF THE WILD

THE ONE SHE LOVED

THE PAINTED LADY

THE MUSKETEERS OF PIG ALLEY

HEREDITY

GOLD AND GLITTER

MY BABY

THE INFORMER

BRUTALITY

THE NEW YORK HAT

MY HERO

THE BURGLAR'S DILEMMA

A CRY FOR HELP

THE GOD WITHIN

1913

THE UNWELCOME GUEST

PIRATE GOLD

THE MASSACRE

OIL AND WATER

THREE FRIENDS

THE TELEPHONE GIRL AND THE
  LADY

FATE

AN ADVENTURE IN THE
  AUTUMN WOODS

A CHANCE DECEPTION

THE TENDERHEARTED BOY

A MISAPPROPRIATED TURKEY

BROTHERS

DRINK'S LURE

LOVE IN AN APARTMENT HOTEL

BROKEN WAYS

A GIRL'S STRATAGEM

NEAR TO EARTH

A WELCOME INTRUDER

THE SHERIFF'S BABY

THE HERO OF LITTLE ITALY

THE PERFIDY OF MARY

A MISUNDERSTOOD BOY

THE LITTLE TEASE

THE LADY AND THE MOUSE

THE WANDERER

THE HOUSE OF DARKNESS

OLAF, AN ATOM

JUST GOLD

HIS MOTHER'S SON

THE YAQUI CUR

THE RANCHERO'S REVENGE

A TIMELY INTERCEPTION

DEATH'S MARATHON

THE SORROWFUL SHORE

THE MISTAKE

THE MOTHERING HEART

HER MOTHER'S OATH

DURING THE ROUNDUP

THE COMING OF ANGELO

AN INDIAN'S LOYALTY

TWO MEN OF THE DESERT

1914

IN PREHISTORIC DAYS, OR WARS
OF THE PRIMAL TRIBES

JUDITH OF BETHULIA

THE BATTLE AT ELDERBUSH
GULCH

THE BATTLE OF THE SEXES

THE ESCAPE

HOME, SWEET HOME

THE AVENGING CONSCIENCE

1915

THE BIRTH OF A NATION

1916

INTOLERANCE

1918

HEARTS OF THE WORLD

THE GREAT LOVE

1919

A ROMANCE OF HAPPY VALLEY

THE GREATEST THING IN LIFE

THE GIRL WHO STAYED HOME

TRUE HEART SUSIE

SCARLET DAYS

BROKEN BLOSSOMS (SARTOV)

THE GREATEST QUESTION

1920

THE IDOL DANCER

THE LOVE FLOWER

WAY DOWN EAST (SARTOV)

1923

THE WHITE ROSE (SARTOV,
SINTZENICH)

1924

AMERICA (SARTOV, LEPICARD,
SINTZENICH)

1927

DRUMS OF LOVE (STRUSS,
JACKSON)

1928

THE BATTLE OF THE SEXES
(STRUSS)

1929

LADY OF THE PAVEMENTS
(STRUSS)

Index